Pressure Canning
Recipe Book

The Ultimate Guide of Home Pressure Canning for Everyone to Enjoy Simple Tasty Canned Food

By Diane Luther

TABLE OF CONTENT

INTRODUCTION......9

CHAPTER 1: Fundamentals of Canning......10

History of Canning......10

Why Pressure Canning?......11

What foods can be pressure canned......13

What foods cannot be pressure canned......13

Does canning affect nutrients......14

CHAPTER 2: Canning 101......16

How to can......16

Tools and Equipment You Must Have......17

Useful Tips and Tricks......19

What Pressure Canner Should You Buy?......20

How to Choose the Suitable Pressure Canner......21

How to Store Home-canned Foods......22

FAQs......23

CHAPTER 3: Beans and Legumes......25

Pressure Canned Baked Beans......25

Pressure-Canned Beans......26

Pressure Canned Pinto Beans......27

Pressure Canned Green Beans......28

Pressure Canned navy dry beans......29

Pressure canned Green peas......30

Canned Garlic Beans......31

Pressure Canned Chickpeas......32

Canned Garlic Garbanzo Beans ···33

Canned Mustard Pork and Beans ·· 33

CHAPTER 4: Vegetables and Tomatoes ···························· **35**

Pressure Canned Potatoes ··· 35

Pressure Canned Carrots ··36

Pressure Canned corn ·· 36

Pressure Canned ASparagus ··37

Pressure Canned Plain Beets ···38

Canned Pumpkin ··· 39

Pressure Canned Hot peppers ·· 40

Pressure Canned Sweet peppers ··· 41

Pressure Canned Sweet Potatoes ··41

Pressure Canned Broccoli ··· 42

Canned Kale ·· 43

Canning Turnips ··· 44

Pressure Canned Caramelized Onions ·······································45

Canned Fiddleheads ·· 46

Pickled Garlic scapes ·· 47

CHAPTER 5: Red Meat, Poultry, Seafood and Games ···········**49**

Pressure Canning Beef Round ··49

Pressure Canned Homemade Chilli ···50

Pressure Canned Beef Short Rib ···51

Pressure Canned Ground Beef ··52

Pressure Canned Stewing Beef ···52

Beef in Wine Sauce ··· 53

Pressure Canned Rosemary Chicken ··· 54

Pressure Canned Chicken Breast ··· 55

Pressure Canned Turkey pieces ··· 56

McDonald's Pressure Canned Fish 57

Pressure Canned Salmon 58

Pressure Canned Tuna 59

Pressure canned Whole clams 59

Pressure Canned Minced Clams 60

Pressure Canned Shrimp 61

Canned Oysters 62

Easy Canned Antelope meat 63

Pressure Canned Deer Meat 64

Canned Beef Stroganoff 65

Peggie's Pressure Canned Deer Meat 66

CHAPTER 6: Soups, Stocks, broths, and stews 67

Canned Vegetable Soup 67

Pressure Canned Chicken Soup 68

Canned Carrot and Ginger Soup 69

Pressure Canned Tomato Soup 70

Canned Chicken Stock 71

American Chicken Stock 72

Home-canned Beef Stock 72

Canned Turkey stock 73

Pressure Canned Turkey Broth 74

Canned Beef Broth 75

Pressure Canned Chicken Broth 76

Pressure Canned Beef Stew 77

Canned Hearty Chili Stew 78

Canned Chili Corn Carne 79

Venison Stew with Veggies 80

CHAPTER 7: Meals in Jar 82

Canned Chicken in jars..82

Corned Beef and Potatoes...82

Canned Hungarian Goulash...83

Pressure canned Garlic Beef Stroganoff.....................84

Pressure Canned Chicken Cacciatore.........................85

Canned Tamales..86

Hamburger Sauce Mix...87

Pressure Canned spicy corn...88

Basic Pork and Beans...89

Canned Dry Kidney beans..90

CHAPTER 8: Pickles Recipes...................................**91**

Canned Pickled Small Beets...91

Pickled Pullet Eggs..92

Pickled Jalapenos..93

Canned Spicy Garlic Pickled Carrots.........................93

Canned Spicy Pickled Asparagus...............................94

Sweet and Spicy Pickled Radishes............................95

Pickled Cherry Tomatoes...96

Canned Garlic Dill Pickles...97

Pickled Cauliflower..98

Pickled Red Grapes..99

CHAPTER 9: James, Jellies and preserve...............**101**

Canned Apple Preserves..101

Canned Apricot Jam...102

Canned Fig Jam..102

Canned Tutti- frutti Jam..103

Grape-Plum Jelly..104

Plum Jelly...105

Canned Strawberry Jelly······································106

Batia Palm Fruit Jelly··107

Pear preserves··108

Watermelon Rind Preserves······························109

CHAPTER 10: Salads and Relishes····················**111**

Canned Zucchini Salad·······································111

Canned Three Bean Salad··································112

Prize Winning Canned Zucchini Relish···············113

Beetroot Relish··114

Spicy Tomato relish···115

Dill Pickle Relish··115

Sweet and Spicy Pickle relish···························116

Canned Pepper Relish······································117

Green Tomato Relish··118

Vidalia Onion Relish···119

CHAPTER 11: Low- Sodium and Low-Sugar Recipes············**120**

Low-Sugar Cucumber slices·····························120

Low- sugar Pickled Beets··································121

Low Sugar Canned Berry syrup························122

Low Sugar Peach-Pineapple spread··················123

Low sugar Grape Jelly with liquid sweetener········124

Low sodium sliced sweet pickles·······················125

Low sodium sweet dill pickles····························126

Low Sugar Canned honey and Cinnamon peaches·······127

Low sugar pears··127

Reduced sugar pears in maple syrup··················128

CHAPTER 12: Fruits···**130**

Brandied Honey and Spice Pears 130

Pressure Canned Apple Pie Filling with Maple and Cinnamon 131

Canned Green Tea Chai- Spiced Peaches 132

Pressure Canned Pickled Plums 133

Canned Spicy Ginger Red Hot Pears 134

Pressure Canned Honey-Lavender Peaches 135

Pressure Canned Caramel Apple Butter 136

Canned Port and Cinnamon Plums 137

Pressure Canned Tomatoes 138

Canned Apple Jam 139

APPENDIX: Measurement Conversion Chart 141

INTRODUCTION

Abundance in fresh vegetables, beans, legumes, and fruits are savored during the high season. Not forgetting beef, seafood, games, and poultry which are sometimes available in plenty for some time. You and your family are able to consume as much as you can, give some to neighbors and friends, and preserve some in the freezer. The challenges come in when the power goes off and doesn't have an alternative power source.

Pressure canning is an opportunity to take control of your food. It is a relatively modern method in the history of preserving food. People have tried drying, using salt, fermenting food long before the recorded history. Preserving foods in jars didn't come until the late 18th century. Unlike all other food preservation methods, the beautifully made jars will give you the satisfaction of knowing that you have food security in your pantry.

Even better, it is a great way to ease your meal planning, minimize what you take to the garbage as well as take a bite in recycling needs. The jars are reusable and can be used as many years as possible. Pressure canning is worth the effort once you look at your highly packed kitchen pantry and have the first bite of the food pressure canned right in your kitchen.

If you are a novice in canning and are looking forward to getting some basic skills, the outline has got you covered. The outline also has some delicious recipes that you can try in your new pressure canner.

CHAPTER 1: Fundamentals of Canning

History of Canning

Canning is a food preservation method in jars that are hermetically sealed. Canning can provide a shelf life of 1-5 years although the time differs under different circumstances. Canned dried lentils, for example, could be edible even after 30 years even though they could have a different appearance, smell and the nutrients content will have deteriorated.

It all started in the French government during the Napoleonic wars when Napoleon Bonaparte offered a hefty reward to anyone who would invent a cheap and convenient way to preserve a large amount of food for navy and army use. In 1809, Nicolas Appert who was a brewer and a french confectioner, in response to the government's call, discovered that cooked food in sealed jars did not spoil unless the seal was leaked.

He, therefore, developed a method of sealing food in a jar or a bottle, heating it to a certain temperature, maintaining the temperature for a certain period of time, then keeping the jar sealed until use. In 1810 Peter Durand patented the use of iron cans which were tin coated. By 1820, he was already supplying the royal navy with canned foods in large quantities. In 1858, John Mason invented a glass container that had a screw-on thread molded on its top and a lid that had a rubber seal.

In the 19th century, Samuel C. Prescott and William Underwood set canning on a scientific basis in the United States. They described specific times, temperatures, and heating requirements to sterilize canned foods. In 1903 Alexander Kerr invented the wide mouth canning jar, an idea that the Ball brothers duplicated. He later invented a metal disk with a gasket that is held in place by a threaded metal ring. This is when the 2 piece canning lid was porn.

Pressure canning technology is still developing and some brands use a single lid that works similarly to the 2 piece lid design.

Why Pressure Canning?

Many people are frightened by pressure canning but they shouldn't be. A pressure canner is easy to use and yield the best results when used correctly. There are also many tutorials on how to use one so make sure you have fundamental knowledge on using it. Below are the reasons why you should pressure can.

Saves your money

If you have a garden and have plenty of harvests, you can preserve veggies and fruits that won't fit in your freezer. Also, if you or your spouse hunt you can preserve as much meat as possible through pressure canning.

Saves time

Pressure canning cuts on the time you need for example to soak beans, so you can get them ready in a stockpot. With canned food, you also don't need to wait for the meat to defrost before cooking dinner.

Saves energy

On top of the pressure canners saving on the time, it also saves energy because a large quantity of food can be preserved in a single batch. You also can warm food in jars which take less energy.

Its eco friendly

Canning food at home instead of buying packed foods in the store reduces food packaging waste for example papers and tins. You also reuse the jars over and over again so the price of shipping the jars is minimal.

Pressure canning allows you to preserve a lot of food at once

You can easily stack your pint jars in the pressure canner letting you can 18 jars at a go. If you have 2 pressure canners running at a go you will double that output. Also, if you get a deal on meat such as game meat or turkeys, you can preserve as much meat as possible all at once through canning.

Pressure canning saves spaces on your fridge or freezer

If you pressure can food from your freezer, you create more space. You can also can food from the harvest instead of preserving them in the fridge. This gives more space in the fridge for other foods that cannot be pressure canned.

Pressure canning fill the pantry with ready to eat meals

Have you ever seen those gorgeous pantry pictures in Pinterest? Those jars must be pressure canned. You can also pressure can as much food as possible to feel your pantry with ready-made food.

Pressure canning will save the day if the electricity goes off

You know how serious it gets when you have perishable foods in the fridge, the power goes off and you don't have a power backup. With pressure canning, food is safe in the jars even when the power goes off.

Canning food saves during a hard economic time

Another major reason to have your pantry packed with canned food is to save you during tough economic times. This may be due to sickness, job loss, death, or even divorce. It's extremely comforting to know that your family will well feed despite a hard time.

Pressure canning is fun and makes great homemade gifts

Trust me shopping for a gift to bring your mother-in-law in your pantry is the best experience. Pressure cooking is also fun and can do it with another person, you can even set goals of how you want your pantry packed with food.

What foods can be pressure canned

The pressure canning method of preserving food is safe for low acid foods. These are foods with a PH of more than 4.6. The foods include meat, seafood, and poultry. Pressure canning these foods prevents the danger of botulism. You can however use a pressure canner as a water bath by replacing the pressure canner lid with an ordinary lid. Add water just like in a water bath then heat the canner as required in the recipe.

What foods cannot be pressure canned

1. Fat-foods with a large amount of fat turn rancid faster than other food. Fat also makes it difficult for the heat to penetrate through every layer giving room for bacteria growth.
2. Dairy- food with dairy products also turn rancid fast. Dairy products have thick consistency so making it hard to properly sterilize them. This gives room for bacteria growth
3. Grains-canning grains are also counterproductive. When you heat grains, you destroy their nutrients. Also, grains do not contain heat well. This makes the inner part of the grain not to be well-heated in order to kill all bacteria.
4. Thickeners- thickeners are added to recipes to give them a thicker consistency. Thickeners turn under extreme heating so they are mostly added to food when ready to be served.
5. Some vegetables- these include broccoli, Brussel sprouts, cabbage, cauliflower, summer squash, olives, lettuce, artichokes, and mashed potatoes.
6. Nuts- nuts have an outer layer of oil they behave the same as fats when canned.
7. Purees- the consistency of puree makes canning dangerous because there no guarantee that all fungi and bacteria will be killed

Does canning affect nutrients

Canned foods are mostly thought to have fewer nutrients than fresh foods. This, however, is not true. In fact, canning has been seen to preserve most nutrients in foods for example carbs, protein, and fats. Most fat-soluble vitamins such as vitamin A,

Vitamin D, Vitamin E, and Vitamin K and minerals are also retained. However, water-soluble vitamins such as vitamin C and vitamin B are sensitive to heat and are damaged. Even better, other healthy compounds in foods may increase. For example, when corn and tomatoes are heated, they release more antioxidants.

CHAPTER 2: Canning 101

How to can

Each brand of pressure canner is slightly different from another so you will need to read the manufacturers' instructions especially if this is your first time in canning. The following instructions apply to pressure canning in general.

Place a rack in the pressure canner and add water.

Each pressure canner comes with a removable rack such that you can pressure can jars when the rack is in place or remove the rack and water bath the jars. Always add 3-inch depth water in the canner or add more if the food will be canned for a long time.

Turn on the heat

If packing the jars with hot food, turn the heat on so that the water can be heated. If packing the food while cold, do not turn the heat on before placing the jars otherwise they will crack.

Fill the jars with food and place in the pressure canner

Fill the clean jars with food but remember to leave a headspace depending on the recipe recommendations. Clean the ar rims, place the lids, and tighten the rings using hands.

Now place the jars in the canner

If you need to stack the jars, make sure to place a rack between them. Stacking allows you to can more jars all at once.

Raise the pressure to process the jars

Depending on the model of your pressure canner, close the petcock or place the weighted gauge on the vent. You will see the pressure start to build up on the dial gauge. When the pressure indicated on the recipe is reached (typically 10 pounds pressure), start to time. Adjust the heat so then the pressure is maintained.

Depressurize the canner before opening the lid.

When the processing time has elapsed, let the pressure canner cool down to depressurize. Do not open the canner until the hissing sound stops.

Open the pressure canner

Carefully open the pressure canner lid by lifting it away from your hands and face. Use a jar lifter to remove the jars from the canner and place on a cooling rack where they will be undisturbed until they are completely cool. Label the jars and store in a cool dry place.

Tools and Equipment You Must Have

If you plan to pressure can food at home there are some special equipment you must have. You don't need as much equipment as you may think. In fact, you will be pleasantly surprised to find out that you already have some of the types of equipment in your kitchen.

A pressure canner

You will need to purchase a canner that is appropriate for you. Also look for a high-quality model and that is easy to use especially if you are new to canning.

Canning jars, lids, and rings

These jars are commonly known as mason are and are made of tempered glass that has the ability to withstand high heat

Tongs

Tongs are like superman's fingers when canning. They are used for reaching on the hot jars without getting burnt. Any variety of tongs in the market will work perfectly.

Jar lifter

Jars lifters are specialized sets of tongs that have rubberized ends that securely fits around any size of canning jars. You can therefore securely lift the jars out of the pressure canner.

Canning funnel

It's not mandatory to have this canning funnel but it helps prevent big mess when packing food in the jars.

A chopstick or a stir stick

This little tool is used to remove air bubbles from the jars. Before sealing your filled jars, slip this stick in the inside edges to get rid of small air bubbles

A stockpot or a Dutch oven

These are used to cook the food you are going to preserve through canning. You may purchase an enameled cast iron Dutch oven that is large for recipes that need big surface area.

A kitchen timer

This is a must-have in the kitchen. You can even buy a digital kitchen timer that will beep when the set time has elapsed.

A slotted spoon

The spoon helps drain off the liquid especially when canning whole fruits or vegetables. The drained liquid is later added to the jars.

Cheesecloth or a strainer

These are very vital, especially when making jellies. They help strain seeds out of the mixture.

Useful Tips and Tricks

Whether you are a gardener, a cook or a homesteader you probably have learned or will learn how to preserve food through canning. These small nuggets of information will help you when home canning foods.

Don't warm your lids ahead of time

It's completely safe to skip heating lids while it's also safe to heat them.   You should never boil the lids. You just need to wash them thoroughly in soapy water.

You also don't need to sterilize canning jars that will you will later process for 10 or more minutes

When the processing time is 10 or more minutes, the jars are sterilized in the process of canning. For jellies that require 5 minutes process time, it won't harm to add the extra 5 minutes so you can skip the sterilization.

Frozen fruits make an amazing jam

There is that pressure that comes with summer large amounts of fresh and ripe fruits from the garden. This protects you from stress overabundant harvest. You can freeze the fruits in the freezer and can them later in the week.

Chopsticks make great bubbling tools

After packing food in the jars, you are required to remove air bubbles trapped in the jars. You can also remove the air bubbles with any narrow utensils in our kitchen. Sharp objects like knives are not suitable since they may etch the glass increasing the chances of breakage.

Don't store the processed jars with bands on

The bands are used to hold the lids in place while processing the jars. Once you are done with processing and the jars are sealed, remove the bands, clean them, dry and store them.

Adjust for altitude

High altitude calls for more pressure. You therefore should increase the pressure but not the cooking time. If not sure of your elevation, always calculate your location altitude for fin results.

What Pressure Canner Should You Buy?

Canning season is around the corner and you are wondering which type of canner to buy and the difference between them.

Water bath canner

The water bath method is a process of processing jars packed with food in boiling water for a particular amount of time depending on the type of food. This method is perfect for high acidic foods like fruits or foods with high added acid like vinegar pickles. A bacteria that causes botulism cannot live in foods with high acidic levels.

Pressure canner

The pressure canning method uses a pressure canner to process jars packed with food. This method is perfect for low acid foods. The high pressure, 240 degrees, in the pressure canner kills the bacteria responsible for botulism. Water boils at 212 degrees under normal conditions so it may not kill all the bacteria's. The good news is a pressure canner can be used as a water bath by simply replacing its lid and adding water to cover the jars by 2 inches.

How to Choose the Suitable Pressure Canner

With the many brands of pressure canner flooding in the market, you should be very careful when choosing the best pressure canner that perfectly suits your personal needs. Below are some factors to consider.

Cost

Let's face it, the price of any commodity always comes into play. This is the foremost factor to consider when making a choice and buying a pressure canner. Do some thorough research on pressure canners in the market, read their reviews in order to make the best decision.

Capacity

The amount of food that canner can pressure can at a go is an essential point to consider. If you need a pressure canner for home use, then buy a small and portable model. If you need a commercial pressure canner, then purchase a larger canner. Commercial canners are however awkward and heavy to handle.

Material

Most pressure canners are made of stainless steel or aluminum. Each has some benefits as well as some drawbacks. Aluminum pressure canners are pocket friendly but are lightweight and don't last for as long as the stainless steel canners. It all depends on your personal needs but I would recommend a stainless steel pressure canner that will last for long.

How to Store Home-canned Foods

Test the seals

After successfully processing jars in the pressure canner, it's always advisable to test the seals to make sure the jars are well-sealed else they food will spoil quickly.

Label jars

Make sure to label all the jars with the contents and date they were processed. Most processed foods last for a year to a year and a half.

Where to store

All jars should be kept in a cool dry place. Avoid direct sunlight or damp places such as near pipes and furnaces that may cause temperature fluctuations

Remove bands

It's wise to remove bands on jars after processing them and before storing them. A lid that is properly sealed will keep food safe and good for as long as it should. A band will also make it difficult to detect food spoilage as a result of improper sealing.

Sort Jars

When storing processed jars on the shelves, make sure to place the older canned jars at the back with the newly canned at the front. This helps use the older ones first.

FAQs

Can a jar be resealed if the lid does not seal correctly?

Yes, canned food can be re-canned if detected within 24 hours. All you need to do is just remove the lid and replace it with another lid. Reprocess the jars at the same pressure and time.

Must I leave a certain headspace in the jar?

Yes, leaving a headspace in a jar is vital to assure a vacuum seal that helps preserve food. A very little headspace may prevent proper sealing. This happens when food bubbles out as air escapes leaving some food particles on the rims that prevent the id from sealing correctly.

Is it important to sterilize jars before canning?

No, jars do not need to be sterilized especially if they are being processed for more than 10 minutes. Jars processed in a water bath, however, for the less than 1o minutes requires sterilization

Can I reuse jar lids?

No, lids should never be used for a second time since after the first processing the sealing compound is indented. This prevents any other airtight seal. Bands may however be reused unless they rust.

Can I can food without salt?

Yes, salt is only used for adding flavor to the food but not to prevent the food from spoiling.

CHAPTER 3: Beans and Legumes

Pressure Canned Baked Beans

These are delicious pressure canned beans which perfectly goes well with lashings of maple syrup or on pancakes

Prep time: 25 minutes, **Cook time:** 10 minutes **Process time** 65 minutes: **Serves** 3 jars

Ingredients

- 1 lb navy beans, dried
- 1 cup onions, finely chopped
- 6 tbsp tomato paste
- 1-1/2 tbsp Worcestershire sauce
- 1-1/2 tbsp mustard powder
- 1-1/2 tbsp salt
- 1-1/2 tbsp black pepper, ground
- 3 tbsp brown sugar
- 1 tbsp kitchen Bouquet
- 2 bay leaves
- 24 oz bean liquid

Preparation Method

1. Put the beans in a pot and add 6 cups of water. Boil the beans for 2 minutes then remove the pot from heat. Let rest for 1 hour while covered.
2. Make the sauce by mixing all other ingredients except the bean liquid and bay leaves in a jug. Set aside.
3. Drain the navy beans and discard the soaking water.
4. Add bay leaves to the pot and cover with 2-5cm water. Bring to boil for 2 minutes then turn off the heat. Drain the water and preserve it then remove the bay leaves and discard them.
5. Take 3 cups of the reserved water and add it to the sauce in the jug. Cover the jug and place it in the microwave for 5 minutes. Remove from the microwave and set aside.
6. Pack the beans in jars leaving a headspace of 3 cm per jar, and then ladle the sauce over the beans maintaining the 3 cm headspace.

7. If you run out of the sauce add the reserved bean stock to the jars.
8. Remove the bubbles, wipe the rims, and put on the lids. Place the jars in the pressure canner.
9. Process the jars at 10 pounds of pressure for 65 minutes. Remove the jars from the canner and place them on a rack to cool.

Calories 119, Total fat 0.5g, Saturated fat 0g, Total carbs 27g, Net carbs 22g Protein 6g, Sugars 0g, Fiber 5g

These are yummy canned beans that every member of your family will love. Ensure you use fresh beans because very old beans will soak up almost all the delicious cooking liquid.

Prep time: 25 minutes, **Cook time:** 30 minutes, **Process time** 75 minutes: **Serves** 3

- 1 lb dried beans
- 1 bay leaf
- 2 quarts water
- Kosher salt

1. Pick through the beans to ensure you pick debris or stones. Wash and rinse the beans well.
2. Put the beans in a bowl with cold water covering them. Soak them overnight.
3. Rinse the beans with clean water and drain them. Add the beans and bay leaf to a stockpot. Add water until covered. Bring the beans to a murmuring boil for 30 minutes.
4. Skim foam on the surface, then pour the beans through coriander to a bowl. Discard the bay leaves and reserve the cooking liquid.
5. Ladle the beans to jars up to 2/3 full then add the cooking liquid leaving 1-inch headspace. Add a half tablespoon of salt on each jar if you desire.
6. Remove any air bubbles and add more cooking liquid if

necessary.

7. Wipe the rims and place the lids on the jars. Place the rings and tighten them. Place the jars in the pressure canner.
8. Process the jars at 10 pounds for 75 minutes. When the time has elapsed, let the pressure reduce to zero and the pressure canner to cool.
9. Remove the jars from the canner and place them on a rack. Label each jar and store in a cool dry place.

Nutritional Information

Calories 114, Total fat 0.5g, Saturated fat 0.1g, Total carbs 20.4g, Net carbs 12.9g Protein 7.6g, Sugars 0g, Fiber 7.5g

Pressure Canned Pinto Beans

These pinto beans are a real lifesaver, especially when preparing frugal dishes. They are filling, packed with nutrients, and versatile. **Prep time:** 25 minutes, **Cook time:** 30 minutes, **Process time:** 75 minutes: **Serves** 6 jars

Ingredients

- 2 lb Pinto beans
- Water
- Salt
- vinegar

Preparation Method

1. Wash your pinto beans and rinse them well. Soak them in water overnight.
2. Rinse the beans and add them to a pot with the water covering the beans by two inches. Bring the beans to boil and stir cook for 30 minutes.
3. Fill your clean jars with beans leaving 1-inch headspace. Add a half tablespoon of salt and vinegar to each pint jar if you desire.
4. Add the cooking liquid in each jar, then release the air bubbles. Add the cooking liquid if necessary.
5. Use a clean and damp towel to wipe the jar rims. Place the lids on the jars then secure the rings

and tighten them. Place the jars in the pressure canner.

6. Process the jars at 10 pounds for 75 minutes. Turn off the heat and let the canner to depressurize.
7. Open the pressure canner and remove the jars. Place them on a rack undisturbed for 24 hours. Remove the rings and store the jars in a cool dry place.

Nutritional Information

Calories 245, Total fat 1g, Saturated fat 0.1g, Total carbs 45g, Net carbs 30g Protein 15g, Sugars 0g, Fiber 15g, sodium 407mg

Pressure Canned Green Beans

The goodness of fresh beans is packed in these pressure canned green beans. They are exemplary delicious plus you get to enjoy green beans even when they are offseason.

Prep time: 45 minutes, **Cook time:** 0 minutes, **Process time:** 20 minutes: **Serves** 3 jars

Ingredients

- 1 lb green beans
- Filtered water
- Seas salt

Preparation Method

1. Wash the beans roughly then use your hands to cut off the tops and bottoms of the beans. Cut the beans into halves.
2. Pack the green beans into your clean jars. You can use pint jars or quart jars. Add a half tablespoon of salt in each jar if using.
3. Boil filtered water in a large kettle and pour the hot water over the beans leaving 1-inch headspace.
4. Use a clean cloth to wipe the rims. Place the lids and the rings then lightly tighten using your hands.
5. Place the jars on a wire rack of the pressure canner and enough water for your canner model.
6. Place the lid and seal it then place it on medium-high heat.
7. Once the valve has released steam for 10 minutes, add the

pressure up to 20 for 25 minutes if using pints and 25 if using quarts.

8. Put off the heat and let the pressure canner depressurize. Carefully remove the jars and place them on a towel undisturbed for 12-24 hours.
9. Transfer them to the storage area.

Nutritional Information

Calories 28, Total fat 0.6g, Saturated fat 0.1g, Total carbs 5.7g, Net carbs 3.1g Protein 1.42g, Sugars 0g, Fiber 2.6g, Potassium 130mg

Pressure Canned navy dry beans

If you don't like or are bored with having refried beans during supper, then these canned navy dry beans are a solid choice for you. It may be complicated to prepare them but they make quick meals pretty easy **Prep time:** 25 minutes, **Cook time:** 30 minutes, **Process time:** 75 minutes: **Serves** 3 jars

Ingredients

- 1 lb navy beans
- Water
- Vinegar
- Lemon juice

Preparation Method

1. Remove any foreign objects from the beans then add them in a bowl with water until covered.
2. Add vinegar and lemon juice in the soaking water and soak overnight.
3. Wash the beans and drain them. Transfer them to a large pot.
4. Cover with 2 inches of water. Bring the beans to boil and frequently stir them.
5. Use a slotted spoon to add the beans in jars preserving the cooking liquid and leaving 1-inch headspace.
6. Add the cooking liquid in the jars maintaining the 1-inch headspace. Wipe the rims and place the lids and the rings on the jars.
7. Place the jars in a pressure canner and process them at 10 pounds for 1 hour 15 minutes for

pints and 1 hour 30 minutes for quarts.

8. Let the canner depressurize to zero before removing the jars. Let all cool and check the lids if they are properly sealed.
9. Store the jars.

Nutritional Information

Calories 127, Total fat 0.6g, Saturated fat 0.1g, Total carbs 23.7g, Net carbs 14.1g Protein 7.5g, Sugars 0g, Fiber 9.6g, Potassium 354mg

Pressure canned Green peas

Pressure canning peas is very easy, unlike beans. They also don't come out marsh and dark as many people fear. They are delicious, appealing, and simply the best compared to store-bought canned peas.

Prep time: 25 minutes, **Cook time:** 35 minutes, **Process time:** 40 minutes: **Serves** 3 jars

Ingredients

- 1 lb dried peas
- Non-iodized salt

Preparation Method

1. Sort the peas to remove any debris.
2. Add the beans in a shallow saucepan and add water. Boil for 2 minutes. Remove From heat and soak the beans for 1 hour while covered.
3. Drain the beans and rinse them with clean water. Add them back to the saucepan and add more water until just covered for. Boil the peas for 30 minutes.
4. Use a slotted spoon to transfer the peas to the jars then add a half tablespoon of non-iodized salt. Add the cooking liquid to each jat and ensure you leave a 1-inch headspace.
5. Use a clean damp cloth to wipe the jar rims then place the lid and rings. Use hands to tighten.
6. Place the jars in the canner and process them at 10 pounds for 40 minutes. Check the canner instructions guide.
7. Let the pressure canner depressurize and cool down before opening it and removing

the jars.

8. Place the jars on a rack undisturbed for 24 hours before transferring them to the storage area.

Nutritional Information

Calories 132, Total fat 0.7g, Saturated fat 0.1g, Total carbs 23.5g, Net carbs 15.2g Protein 8.8g, Sugars 9.2g, Fiber 8.3g

Canned Garlic Beans

Cooking beans in the Crockpot and freezing them in a freezer is much easier than canning them. However, if the power goes off all will be a total loss. That's why you should consider canning your beans.

Prep time: 45 minutes, **Cook time:** 30 minutes, **Process time:** 60 minutes: **Serves** 3 jars

Ingredients

- 2-1/4 lb dried black beans
- Salt
- Water
- A handful cilantro
- 5 garlic cloves, diced

Preparation Method

1. Sort the beans to remove any unwanted particles.
2. Place the beans in a large pan and cover them in water, about 2 inches.
3. Place the pan on the heat and bring the water and beans to boil for 2 minutes.
4. Remove the beans from heat and let soak covered for 1 hour. Drain the water and return the pan back on the heat.
5. Add more water until just covered. Add cilantro and garlic. bring the beans and water to boil for 30 minutes.
6. Use a slotted spoon to pack the beans in jars leaving 1-inch headspace. Add 1/2 tablespoon of salt to each jar then add the cooking liquid to cover the beans.
7. Remove the bubbles, wipe the jar rims, place the lid and rings on and use hands to tighten.
8. Process the jars for 60 minutes at 10 pounds pressure. Wait for the canner to depressurize before removing the jars and

storing them.

Nutritional Information

Calories 147, Total fat 0g, Saturated fat 0g, Total carbs 13g, Net carbs 8g Protein 5g, Sugars 0g, Fiber 5g, Sodium 10mg, Potassium 233mg

Pressure Canned Chickpeas

Chickpeas are among the most common staple foods in many cultures. They are delicious and go perfectly with a wide range of side dishes. Even better, these pressure canned chickpeas are the easiest to prepare.

Prep time: 25 minutes, **Cook time:** 30 minutes, **Process time:** 60 minutes: **Serves** 5-pint jars

Ingredients

- 2-1/4 lb chickpeas
- Salt
- Water

Preparation Method

1. Wash the chickpeas and cover them with water in a pan. Bring them to boil for 2 minutes. Remove the chickpeas from heat and soak them for an hour.
2. Drain the chickpeas and add more water to just cover them. Boil the chickpeas for 30 minutes.
3. Pack the chickpeas in jars leaving 1-inch headspace. Add a half tablespoon salt in each jar then add cooking liquid to cover the beans.
4. Remove the air bubble and wipe the jar rims. Place the lids and rings on.
5. Process the pint jars for 60 minutes in the pressure canner at 10 pounds pressure.
6. Wait for the pressure canner to depressurize before removing the jars.

Nutritional Information

Calories 269, Total fat 4g, Saturated fat 0.1g, Total carbs 45g, Net carbs 33g Protein 15g, Sugars 7g, Fiber 12g

Canned Garlic Garbanzo Beans

If you love to make homemade hummus then you will need to pressure these garbanzo beans, so that you always have them around.

Prep time: 25 minutes, **Cook time:** 2 minutes, **Process time:** 75 minutes: **Serves** 9 jars

Ingredients

- 6 cups garbanzo beans
- 18 garlic cloves
- 3 tbsp salt

Preparation Method

1. Add the beans in a stockpot such that the water is 2 inches above the beans. Place the pot over heat and bring the beans to boil for 2 minutes.
2. Remove the pot from heat and let the beans soak in water for 1 hour.
3. Use a slotted spoon to pack the beans in jars filling the jars up to 3/4 full.
4. Add 2 garlic cloves and a 1/4 tablespoon of salt in each jar. Add the cooking liquid in each jar and if not enough add hot water.
5. Wipe the jar rims with a clean damp towel then place the lids and rings on the jars.
6. Process the jars in the pressure canner at 10 pounds for 75 minutes.
7. Wait for the pressure canner to depressurize before removing the jars.

Nutritional Information

Calories 268, Total fat 5g, Saturated fat 0.1g, Total carbs 46g, Net carbs 34g Protein 15g, Sugars 7g, Fiber 13g

Canned Mustard Pork and Beans

These beans are deliciously nice

and soft. They are very easy to make and will be loved by every member of your family.

Prep time: 25 minutes, **Cook time:** 30 minutes, **Process time:** 75 minutes: **Serves** 3 jars

Ingredients

- 2 lb navy beans
- 2 onions, chopped
- 8 pieces salt pork
- 1/4 cup brown sugar
- 1 tbsp yellow mustard
- 2 tbsp honey
- 30 oz tomato sauce
- 3 cups water
- 1 tbsp salt

Preparation Method

1. Preheat your pressure canner.
2. Place a half cup of navy beans in each jar. Divide the onions equally among the jars then add a piece of pork to each jar.
3. Heat a saucepan and add sugar, mustard, honey, tomato sauce, and water. Bring the mixture to boil. Ladle the sauce mixture to each jar.
4. Fill the jar with boiling water ensuring you leave 1-inch headspace.
5. Wipe the jar rims and place the lids and rings on the jars. Place the jars in the pressure canner and process at 10 pounds for 75 minutes.
6. Wait for the pressure canner to depressurize before removing the jars. Store in a cool dry place for up to a year.

Nutritional Information

Calories 130, Total fat 1g, Saturated fat 0g, Total carbs 26g, Net carbs 20g Protein 5g, Sugars 8g, Fiber 6g, Sodium 440mg, Potassium 260mg

Pressure Canned Potatoes

Pressure canned potatoes are delicious, versatile, and very easy to make. They are perfect for roasts, stews, or soups while making quick meals.

Prep time: 35 minutes, **Cook time:** 0 minutes, **Process time:** 40 minutes: **Serves** 7-quart jars

Ingredients

- 6 lb white potatoes
- Canning salt

Preparation Method

1. Wash the jars thoroughly then place then in a cold oven. Heat it to 250°F.
2. Meanwhile, bring water in a pot to boil. Also, add 4 inches of water in the pressure canner and place it over medium heat.
3. Peel the potatoes, wash them and cut into 2 inches pieces.
4. Add a tablespoon of salt in each jar then fill with potatoes leaving a 1-inch headspace. Pour the boiling water in each jar then use a canning knife to remove the air bubbles from the jars.
5. Wipe the jar rims and place the lids and rings on the jars. Place the jars in the pressure canner and secure the lid according to the manufacture instructions.
6. Process the jars at 10 pounds for 40 minutes and 35 minutes for pit jars.
7. Turn off the heat and let the canner depressurize before removing the jars. Place the jars on a towel undisturbed for 24 minutes.
8. Store in a cool dry place.

Nutritional Information

Calories 108, Total fat 0.4g, Saturated fat 0.1g, Total carbs 24.5g, Net carbs 20.4g Protein 2.5g,

Sugars 2g, Fiber 4.1g, Sodium 394.2mg, Potassium 412.2mg

Pressure Canned Carrots

If you have raised more than enough carrots in your garden and are wondering how to freshly preserve them for a really long time, look no further. Pressure canning the carrots is a wise idea.

Prep time: 35 minutes, **Cook time:** 0 minutes, **Process time:** 40 minutes: **Serves** 7-quart jars

Ingredients

- 2-1/2 lb Carrots
- Salt
- water

Preparation Method

1. Wash the carrots and trim them. Peel the carrots and wash them again if you desire.
2. Slice the carrots into pieces of your liking.
3. Pack the carrots in the jars leaving a 1-inch headspace. Add a 1/2 tablespoon of salt to each jar then add boiling water to each jar.
4. Remove the air bubbles and add more hot water if necessary. Wipe the jar rims with a clean damp towel, then place the lids on the jars.
5. Place the jars in the pressure canner and process them for 25 minutes at 10 pounds pressure.
6. Let the canner rest and depressurize before removing the jar.

Nutritional Information

Calories 27, Total fat 0.1g, Saturated fat 0g, Total carbs 6.4g, Net carbs 4.1g Protein 2.5g, Sugars 2.7g, Fiber 2.3g, Sodium 45mg

Pressure Canned corn

These canned corns are irresistibly delicious and once you can them, you will want to do it more and more.

Everyone in your family will love these corn..

Prep time: 35 minutes, **Cook time:** 0 minutes, **Process time:** 55 minutes: **Serves** 5 quart jars

Ingredients

- 2lb Fresh corn
- Water
- salt

Preparation Method

1. Cut off the corn from the cob and bring water to boil.
2. Pack the corn kernels in the jars and leave a 1-inch headspace. Add a half tablespoon of salt on each jar then add the boiled water to cover the corn.
3. Remove any air bubble and add more water if necessary.
4. Wipe the rims and place the lids and rings on the jars. Transfer the jars to the pressure canner and process them at 10 pounds pressure for 55 minutes.
5. Let the canner depressurize before removing the jars. Store in a cool dry place.

Nutritional Information

Calories 177, Total fat 3.2g, Saturated fat 0.7g, Total carbs 38g, Net carbs 32.7g Protein 6g, Sugars 12g, Fiber 5.3g, Sodium 540mg, Potassium 348mg

Pressure Canned ASparagus

Pressure canning asparagus is so easy that you can preserve as much as possible and enjoy asparagus all year round. Canned asparagus is so delicious that you will want to eat more and more of them.

Prep time: 35 minutes, **Cook time:** 0 minutes, **Process time:** 30 minutes: **Serves** 9-quart jars

Ingredients

- 10 lb asparagus
- Canning salt
- Boiling water

Preparation Method

1. Bring water to boil in a pot over high heat.
2. Trim the asparagus such that they fit in the jars. Pack them in the jars, add 1/2 tablespoon salt

and the boiling water leaving a 1-inch headspace.

3. Wipe the jar rims, place the lids, place the rings, and use hands to tighten.
4. Place the jars in the pressure canner and process at 10 pounds for 30 minutes for pints and 40 minutes for quarts.
5. Allow the pressure canner to depressurize completely before removing the jars.

Nutritional Information

Calories 20, Total fat 0g, Saturated fat 0g, Total carbs 3g, Net carbs 2g Protein 2g, Sugars 1g, Fiber 1g, Sodium 430mg

Pressure Canned Plain Beets

These pressure canned plain beets are extremely delicious. What an awesome treat to toss these beets with some oil or duck fat then roast in the microwave for a few seconds or zap the beets in the oven and serve with a sprinkle of dill and sour cream.

Prep time: 35 minutes, **Cook time:** 0 minutes, **Process time:** 40 minutes: **Serves** 3-quart jars

Ingredients

- 1 lb Beets
- Water
- Pickling salt

Preparation Method

1. Trim the tops of the beets leaving an inch long top. Also, leave the roots on the beets.
2. Wash the beets thoroughly with clean water then put them in a pot.
3. Cover the beets with water and bring to boil for 15-25 minutes or until the skin can come out easily.
4. Remove the beets from hot water and let them cool a little bit such that you can hold them. They should be at least warm when being put in the jar.
5. Trim the remaining stem and roots then peel the beets.
6. Slice the beets into large slices leaving the small ones whole. Put the beets in jars and leave a 1-inch headspace.

7. Add a half tablespoon of salt in each jar then add boiling water in each jar.
8. Remove any bubbles in the jar then wipe the rims with a clean piece of cloth.
9. Put on the lids and the rings. Process the jars at 10 pounds for 30 minutes.
10. Let the pressure canner depressurize to zero before removing the jars.

Calories 58, Total fat 0.2g, Saturated fat 0.1g, Total carbs 13g, Net carbs 9.2g Protein 2.2g, Sugars 9.2g, Fiber 3.8g

Canned Pumpkin

If you are a pumpkin puree lover, then this canned pumpkin is a great idea to add in your kitchen pantry. When you need to make a pie, just open a jar, strain the pumpkin, and there you go!

Prep time: 35 minutes, **Cook time:** 0 minutes, **Process time:** 40 minutes: **Serves** 3quart jars

Ingredients

- 1 lb Pie pumpkins
- Water

Preparation Method

1. Start by cutting out the stem as if you want to use the pumpkin to curve, then cut it into 4 equal wedges.
2. Scrape out the seeds then use a knife to peel the pumpkin. Slice the pumpkin into 1-inch cubes.
3. Place the pumpkin cubes in a large pot and water until the pumpkin is just covered.
4. Bring the pumpkin and water to boil for 2 minutes. Carefully transfer the pumpkin pieces into jars making sure you avoid smashing them.
5. Fill each jar with the cooking liquid leaving 1-inch headspace. Wipe the jar rims with a clean damp piece of cloth.
6. Place the lids and rings on the jars and place them in the pressure canner.
7. Process the jars for at 15 pounds pressure for 90 minutes for quart jars and for 55 minutes

for pint jars.

8. Wait until the pressure canner has depressurized to zero before removing the jars.

Nutritional Information

Calories 49, Total fat 0g, Saturated fat 0g, Total carbs 12g, Net carbs 9g Protein 2g, Sugars 2g, Fiber 3g

Pressure Canned Hot peppers

If you are a hot pepper lover and have a great harvest from your farm that can sustain you up to a year, here is a great solution. Pressure can the hot peppers and store them in a cool dry place

Prep time: 35 minutes, **Cook time:** 10 minutes, **Process time:** 35 minutes: **Serves** 2-pint jars

Ingredients

- 2 lb hot peppers
- salt

Preparation Method

1. Wear rubber gloves on your hands to avoid burning sensation.

2. Sort the peppers and select the fresh and firm once for maximum results.

3. Wash the hot peppers and place them on a lined baking sheet in a single layer.

4. Broil in the broiler for 5-10 minutes making sure you flip over once.

5. Transfer the hot pepper to a zip lock bag and seal tightly. Let rest for 10 minutes then remove them from the bag. Rub off as much peppers skin as much as possible.

6. Trim the tops off, scrape out the seeds, then cut the peppers into two or into sizes that will fit in the jar.

7. Pac the peppers in the jars then add a half tablespoon of salt to each jar. Add boil water to each bar leaving a 1-inch headspace.

8. Wipe the rims, close the lids and place the rings in place. Process the jars for 35 minutes at 10 pounds pressure.

9. Wait for the scanner to depressurize before removing the jars out.

Nutritional Information

Calories 6 Total fat 0.1g, Saturated fat 0g, Total carbs 1.3g, Net carbs 1.1g Protein 0.3g, Sugars 0.8g, Fiber 0.2g

Pressure Canned Sweet peppers

These sweet peppers are delicious and versatile. They can be used in stews, soups, skillet meals. canned sweet peppers will be good for up to an year even though their quality degrades with time.

Prep time: 35 minutes, **Cook time:** 3 minutes, **Process time:** 35 minutes: **Serves** 2 pint jars

Ingredients

- 2 lb sweet bell peppers
- salt

Preparation Method

1. Thoroughly wash the sweet bell peppers then cut them into quarters.
2. Place the peppers in a pot covered with water and bring to boil for 3 minutes.
3. Transfer the peppers in the pint jars then add a quarter tablespoon salt in each jar.
4. Ladle the cooking liquid in each jar leaving 1-inch headspace. Wipe the rims and place the lids and rings.
5. Place the jars in the pressure canner and process for 35 minutes at 10 pounds pressure.
6. Let the pressure canner depressurize before removing the jars.

Nutritional Information

Calories 46, Total fat 0.4g, Saturated fat 0g, Total carbs 9.4g, Net carbs 6.3g Protein 1.5g, Sugars 0g, Fiber 3.1g, Sodium 6mg, Potassium 314mg

Pressure Canned Sweet Potatoes

I love sweet potatoes. Who doesn't

love sweet potatoes? Sweet potatoes are so yummy that you will want to eat them for breakfast, lunch and even dinner. Make sure to pack in enough in jars to take you all year long when they are on season.

Prep time: 35 minutes, **Cook time:** 0 minutes, **Process time:** 40 minutes: **Serves** 10-quart jars

Ingredients

- 10 lb sweet potatoes
- Water
- 1-1/2 cup sugar

Preparation Method

1. Add the whole sweet potatoes in a stockpot, then add water until they are covered. Bring to boil for 15 minutes.
2. Remove the sweet potatoes from water and let them cool so that they are easy to peel.
3. Cut them into large chunks then pack them in the clean jars leaving a half-inch headspace.
4. Bring to boil 3 cups of water and add 1-1/2 cups of brown sugar until the sugar has dissolved.
5. Add boiled water to some of the jars and simple brown sugar syrup to others but maintain the headspace. Remove the bubble and add more hot water if necessary.
6. Wipe the jar rims then palace the lids and rings on. Place the jars in the canner and process for at 10 pounds for 90 minutes for quart jars and 65 minutes for pint jars.
7. Let the pressure drop so that you can remove the jars from the canner.

Nutritional Information

Calories 86, Total fat 0.1g, Saturated fat 0g, Total carbs 20.1g, Net carbs 17.1g Protein 1.6g, Sugars 4.2g, Fiber 3g

Pressure Canned Broccoli

It's no secret that you need to take a lot of vegetables for health purposes. Broccoli is one of the most nutritious vegetables that you need to have in your kitchen pantry all year round

Prep time: 35 minutes, **Cook time:** 3

minutes, **Process time:** 30 minutes: **Serves** 4-pint jars

Ingredients

- 4 lb fresh broccoli
- Canning salt
- water

Preparation Method

1. Soak then thoroughly wash the broccoli to remove all the dirt that could be in the head.
2. Cut the head into 2-inch pieces and discard the stems. You can also can the stems if you desire.
3. Place the broccoli in boiling water and let it boil for 3 minutes.
4. Use a slotted spoon to pack the broccoli in sterilized jars then add the hot water in each jar leaving 1-inch headspace. Release any air bubbles in each jar and add the water if necessary.
5. Add 1 tablespoon of canning salt to each jar then wipe the rims with a clean towel. Place the lids and rings then transfer the jars to the pressure canner.
6. Process the jars at 10 pounds for 30 minutes. Let the canner depressurize before removing the jars.
7. Let the jars rest overnight to store them in a cool dry place.

Nutritional Information

Calories 8, Total fat 0.1g, Saturated fat 0g, Total carbs 1.5g, Net carbs 0.9g Protein 0.6g, Sugars 0.4g, Fiber 0.6g, Sodium 589.2mg, Potassium 72mg

Canned Kale

During winter, there is plenty of kale in most gardens. You make kale chips, you steam the kale and even feed the poultry but it is still in surplus. To pave way for other crops in the garden, you need to cut the kale and preserve them in jars for later.

Prep time: 35 minutes, **Cook time:** 10 minutes, **Process time:** 70 minutes: **Serves** 5-pint jars

Ingredients

- 10 lb Kale
- water

1. Chop the kale into bite-size pieces then remove all the hard stems and yellow parts of the kale.
2. Rinse the kale to remove any dirt then add it to the stockpot. Cover the kale with water.
3. Bring the water to boil until the kale has wilted nicely.
4. Use a slotted spoon to full the jars with kale then add 1/2 tablespoon salt in each jar. Add the cooking liquid and leave a 1-inch headspace.
5. Remove any air bubble and add more cooking liquid if necessary. Wipe the rims and place the lids and rings on the jars.
6. Process the jars at 10-11 pounds of pressure for 70 minutes. Turn off the heat and let the canner cool before using a jar lifer to remove the jars.
7. Let rest for 24 hours undisturbed before storing them in a cool dry place.

Nutritional Information

Calories 85, Total fat 0.5g, Saturated fat 0.1g, Total carbs 6.7g, Net carbs 5.4g Protein 2.2g, Sugars 0g, Fiber 1.3g, Sodium 28.8mg, Potassium 299mg

Canning Turnips

Turnips are wonderfully tender and make a perfect vegetable side dish of all times of the year. All you need is to toss the canned chunks of turnips in oil and spices then bake in the oven.

Prep time: 35 minutes, **Cook time:** 10 minutes, **Process time:** 30 minutes: **Serves** 12-pint jars

Ingredients

- 10 lb turnips
- water

Preparation Method

1. Peel the turnips then dice them into small pieces
2. Add the turnips in a stockpot and add cold water until just covered. Drain the water to get lid of dirt and debris.

3. Cover with water once more and bring them to boil over medium-high heat. Reduce heat and let simmer for 5 minutes.
4. Use a slotted spoon to transfer the hot turnips in sterilized jars. Fill the jar with the cooking liquid leaving 1-inch headspace. Add a half tablespoon of pickling salt.
5. Remove any air bubble and add the cooking liquid if necessary. Wipe the pint jars and place the lids and rings.
6. Load the jars into the pressure canner and process at 10 pounds for 30 minutes.
7. Allow the canner to depressurize to zero before removing the jars.

Nutritional Information

Calories 36.4, Total fat 0.13g, Saturated fat 0g, Total carbs 8.36g, Net carbs 20.4g Protein 1.17g, Sugars 1g, Fiber 2.34g, Sodium 87.1mg

Pressure Canned Caramelized Onions

There is nothing delicious than these caramelized onions on a beef sandwich, baked potatoes or when mashed into potatoes

Prep time: 35 minutes, **Cook time:** 10 hours, **Process time:** 70 minutes: **Serves** 6-pint jars

Ingredients

- 6 lb Onions
- 2 stick butter
- water

Preparation Method

1. Peel the onions and slice them into 1/4 inches slices.
2. Melt 1 stick of butter in the stockpot over high heat then add the diced onions.
3. Slice another stick of butter over the onions. Cook on high for an hour until the butter has melted

and the onions were sweating a little bit.

4. Reduce the heat and let cook for 10 hours or overnight while stirring occasionally. The onions should be golden brown and well caramelized.
5. Ladle the onions in the sterilized hot jars then remove any air bubbles. Wipe the jar rims with a damp clean cloth
6. Place the lid and rings on the jars and process them at 10 pounds pressure for 70 minutes.
7. Remove the pressure canner from heat and let its pressure reduce to zero before removing the jars.

Nutritional Information

Calories 178, Total fat 12g, Saturated fat 2g, Total carbs 13g, Net carbs 11g Protein 1g, Sugars 6g, Fiber 2g, Sodium 394mg, Potassium 214mg

Canned Fiddleheads

These are delicious vegetables that are rare in the vegetable stores. They are mildly toxic when raw so need to be boiled in saltwater then rinsed well to get the last bit of the toxins

Prep time: 35 minutes, **Cook time:** 10 minutes, **Process time:** 50 minutes: **Serves** 1-pint jars

Ingredients

- 2 cups fiddleheads
- 1/2 cup of water
- 1/2 cup white vinegar
- 1 tbsp salt
- 1/2 tbsp peppercorns
- 1/2 tbsp fennel
- 1/2 tbsp coriander
- 1 sprig thyme
- 3 garlic cloves

Preparation Method

1. Trim off the cut ends then boil the fiddleheads for 10 minutes in salted water.

2. Strain the fiddleheads and rinse them with clean water. Pack the fiddleheads in the jars and leave 1-inch headspace.
3. Add the spices directly in each jar on top of the fiddleheads.
4. Boil water, vinegar, and salt in a saucepan and pour over the fiddleheads.
5. Wipe the rims, then place the lids and the rings on the jars. Place the jars in the pressure canner and process at 10 pounds pressure for 10 minutes.

Nutritional Information

Calories 22, Total fat 0.2g, Saturated fat 0g, Total carbs 3g, Net carbs 3g Protein 2.8g, Sugars 1g, Fiber 1g

Pickled Garlic scapes

If you grow garlic, you will realize that it's hard to use all the garlic scrapes when fresh. That why you should pressure them to freshly preserve them. Garlic scrapes are perfect for scrambled eggs and make an awesome fresh garlic scrape pesto.

Prep time: 5 minutes, **Cook time:** 10 minutes, **Process time:** 55 minutes: **Serves** 3-pint jars

Ingredients

- 1 lb garlic scrapes
- 3 tbsp dill seed
- 1-1/2 tbsp whole peppercorns
- 1-1/2 tbsp whole coriander
- 1-1/2 cups apple cider vinegar
- 1-1/2 cup water
- 2 tbsp pickling salt

Preparation Method

1. Trim the scrapes to remove the blossoms and the tough bottom end. Reserve the blossoms for another use.
2. Cut the scrapes to a size that will fit the jars. Pack the scrapes in the jars then add a tablespoon of dill, 1/2 tablespoon peppercorn, and coriander seeds in each jar. You can also add red pepper flakes for spicy pickles.
3. Mix vinegar, water, and salt in a pot then bring the mixture to boil while stirring until the salt has dissolved.

4. Pour the hot mixture over the garlic scrapes in the jars leaving 1-inch headspace.
5. Wipe the rim of the jars with a damp cloth then place the lids and rings.
6. Place the jars in the pressure canner and process for 55 minutes at 10 pounds pressure.
7. Let the canner depressurize to zero before removing the jars. Transfer the jars to a rack and let them rest for 24 hours undisturbed.
8. Store the jars in a cool dry place.

Nutritional Information

Calories 20, Total fat 0g, Saturated fat 0g, Total carbs 4g, Net carbs 4g Protein 1g, Sugars 0g, Fiber 0g.

CHAPTER 5: Red Meat, Poultry, Seafood and Games

Pressure Canning Beef Round

Pressure canning beef rounds is surprisingly easy. The big secret is to brown the meat so that the pieces do not stick together when canned.

Prep time: 60 minutes, **Cook time:** 5 minutes, **Process time:** 60 minutes: **Serves** 1

- Beef round
- Cooking spray
- Water
- salt

1. Trim any gristle from the beef then cut it into cubes.
2. Heat a non-stick skillet over medium heat and spray it with cooking spray brown the beef rounds in batches and transfer them to a covered bowl to keep them hot.
3. Pack the beef in 1/2 litre jars leaving 1-inch headspace. Add a 1/2 tablespoon of salt to each jar.
4. Add boiling water or stock maintaining the 1-inch headspace.
5. Wipe the rims and place the lids on. Transfer the jars to the pressure canner and process them at 10 pounds for 75 minutes.
6. Wait for the pressure canner to depressurize to zero before removing the jars.

7. Place the jars on a cooling rack for 12-24 hours then store in a cool dry place.

Nutritional Information

Calories 94, Total fat 1.8g, Saturated fat 0.6g, Total carbs 0g, Net carbs 0g Protein 18.8g, Sugars 0g, Fiber 0g, Sodium 59mg, Potassium 0mg

Pressure Canned Homemade Chilli

This is the most amazing canned chili I have ever made. It is packed with flavors, nutrients and every member of my family, even the picky eaters, love it.

Prep time: 15 minutes, **Cook time:** 15 minutes, **Process time:** 75 minutes: **Serves** 12 pints

Ingredients

- 3 cups kidney beans
- 5 tbsp salt
- 3 lb beef, ground
- 1-1/2 cup onion, chopped
- 1 cup bell peppers, chopped
- 3-6 tbsp chili seasoning mix
- 1 tbsp black pepper
- 8 cups tomatoes, chopped
- 4 cups tomato juice
- 15 oz tomato sauce

Preparation Method

1. Wash beans in clean water and rinse them. Put the beans in a stockpot and cover them with water, 2 inches above the beans. Let the beans soak overnight.
2. Rinse the beans and add more water with 2 tablespoon salt. Heat the beans and water until simmering, then cook for 30 minutes. Drain the beans.
3. Brown beef, onions, and bell peppers in a large skillet. Transfer them o a large pot then add the beans.
4. . Add seasoning mix, black pepper, tomatoes, tomato sauce, and tomato juice to the pot and simmer for 5 minutes.
5. Ladle the mixture to the sterilized jars leaving 1-inch headspace. Wipe the rims and place the lid and rings on the jars
6. Process the jars at 11 pounds pressure for 75 minutes. Wait for

the canner to cool to remove the jars.

7. Place the jars on a cooling rack until the lids seal

Nutritional Information

Calories 452, Total fat 15g, Saturated fat 3.6g, Total carbs 40g, Net carbs 27g Protein 43g, Sugars 8.4g, Fiber 13g, Sodium 755mg, Potassium 1377mg

Pressure Canned Beef Short Rib

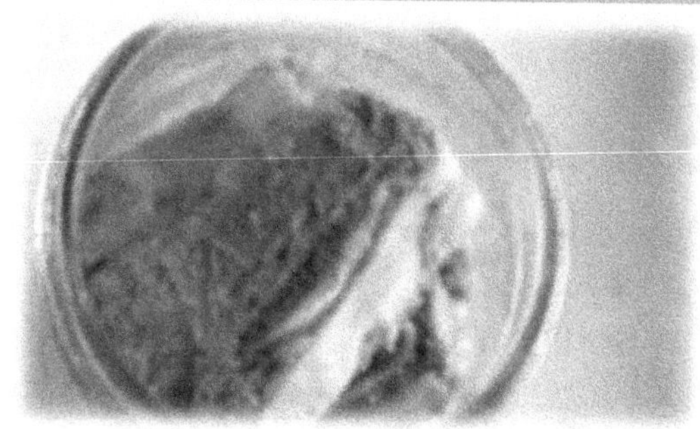

Pressure canning short ribs gives them some deep beefy flavors that are irresistible. Don't forget to warn the diners that there may be bones in the meat even if it may seem obvious.

Prep time: 60 minutes, **Cook time:** 5 minutes, **Process time:** 75 minutes: **Serves** 12 pints

Ingredients

- 10 lb Beef short rib
- Water
- Pickling salt

Preparation Method

1. Heat a skillet sprayed with cooking spray. Brown the ground beef and keep it covered in a bowl to keep it hot.
2. Pack the beef in sterilized jars leaving a 1-inch headspace. Add a 1/2 tablespoon of pickling salt in each jar.
3. Add boiling water or stock to each jar, then remove the bubbles.
4. Wipe the rims and place the lids on. Transfer the jars to the pressure canner and process them at 10 pounds for 75 minutes.
5. Wait for the pressure canner to depressurize to zero before removing the jars.
6. Place the jars on a cooling rack for 24 hours then store in a cool dry place.

Nutritional Information

Calories 205, Total fat 9g, Saturated fat 3.4g, Total carbs 0g, Net carbs 0g Protein 28.9g, Sugars 0g, Fiber 0g, Sodium 60mg, Potassium 363mg

Pressure Canned Ground Beef

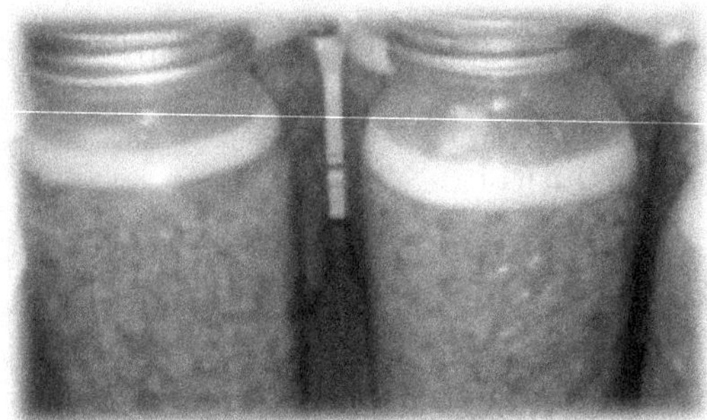

If you are a taco lover then consider adding this pressure canned ground beef in your kitchen pantry. The ground beef also goes perfectly with casseroles, stir-fried rice or noodle dishes.

Prep time: 50 minutes, **Cook time:** 5 minutes, **Process time:** 60 minutes: **Serves** 12 pints

Ingredients

- 12 lb Ground beef
- Water
- salt

Preparation Method

1. Heat a skillet sprayed with cooking spray. Brown the ground and keep it in a covered bowl to keep them hot.
2. Pack the beef in sterilized jars leaving a 1-inch headspace. Add a 1/2 tablespoon of pickling salt in each jar.
3. Add boiling water or stock, then remove the bubbles.
4. Wipe the rims and place the lids on. Transfer the jars to the pressure canner and process them at 10 pounds for 75 minutes.
5. Wait for the pressure canner to depressurize to zero before removing the jars.
6. Place the jars on a cooling rack for 24 hours then store in a cool dry place.

Nutritional Information

Calories 124, Total fat 4g, Saturated fat 1.8g, Total carbs 0g, Net carbs 0g Protein 21.2g, Sugars 0g, Fiber 0g, Sodium 62mg, Potassium 0mg

Pressure Canned Stewing Beef

Pressure canning stewed beef gives it a deep flavor and a melt in the mount texture that everyone will love. **Prep time:** 60 minutes, **Cook time:** 5 minutes, **Process time:** 75 minutes: **Serves** 5 pints

- 5 lb Stewing beef
- Water
- Pickling salt

Preparation Method

1. Trim any gristle on the stewed beef then cut it into strips or into cubes
2. Heat a skillet sprayed with cooking spray. Brown the stewed beef in batches and keep it in a covered bowl to keep them hot.
3. Pack the beef in sterilized jars leaving 1-inch headspace. Add a 1/2 tablespoon of pickling salt in each jar.
4. Add boiling water or stock, then remove the bubbles.
5. Wipe the rims and place the lids on. Transfer the jars to the pressure canner and process them at 10 pounds for 75 minutes.
6. Wait for the pressure canner to depressurize to zero before removing the jars.
7. Place the jars on a cooling rack for 24 hours then store in a cool dry place.

Nutritional Information

Calories 186, Total fat 6.2g, Saturated fat 2.4g, Total carbs 0g, Net carbs 0g Protein 30.3g, Sugars 0g, Fiber 0g, Sodium 66mg, Potassium 403mg

Beef in Wine Sauce

This mouthwatering beef in wine sauce is truly a luxurious treat for your friends coming over for dinner Serve the beef with squash, potato, or carrot mash.
Prep time: 40 minutes, **Cook time:** 60 minutes, **Process time:** 75 minutes: **Serves** 3 pints

Ingredients

- 5 oz apple

- 4 oz carrot, shredded
- 3/4 cup onions
- 2 lb stewing beef
- 3/4 cup of water
- 1/2 cup red wine
- 1 tbsp salt
- 2 garlic cloves
- 2 beef bouillon cubes
- 2 bay leaves
- 1/2 tbsp kitchen bouquet

Preparation Method

1. Wash the apples thoroughly then core and shred them. Put them in a large pot.
2. Wash the carrots and peel them. Wash once more and shred them. Add them to the pot too.
3. Wash onions, peel and slice them into small pieces. Add the onions to the pot.
4. Cut the stewing beef into an inch size pieces and brown it on a skillet in batches over medium heat. Add the beef to the pot.
5. Add all other ingredients to the pot. Bring everything to boil then reduce heat to low and simmer for 1 hour or until the meat is tender.
6. Remove the bay leaves and discard them. Ladle the mixture in sterilized jars leaving an inch headspace.
7. Remove the bubbles then wipe the rims with a clean damp towel.
8. Put on the lids and the rings on the jars. Transfer the jars to the pressure canner and process them at 10 pounds pressure for 75 minutes.
9. Wait for the pressure canner to depressurize to zero before removing the jars.
10. Place the jars on a cooling rack for 24 hours then store in a cool dry place.

Nutritional Information

Calories 364, Total fat 10.7g, Saturated fat 3.3g, Total carbs 12.1g, Net carbs 10g Protein 49.1g, Sugars 7.7g, Fiber 2.1g, Sodium 709mg, Potassium 826mg

Pressure Canned Rosemary Chicken

This pressure canned rosemary chicken is an awesome gourmet

side dish to any food. Its easy and fast since no thawing is required.
Prep time: 40 minutes, **Cook time:** 5 minutes, **Process time:** 60 minutes: **Serves** 10 pints

Ingredients

- 20 2- inch sprigs of rosemary
- 10 lb chicken breast, boneless and skinless
- 1/4 cup salt

Preparation Method

1. Add a sprig of rosemary to each sterilized jar.
2. Cut the chicken breasts into large chunks and pack in the jars leaving a 1-1/2 inches headspace.
3. Add a sprig of rosemary at the top then add a tablespoon of salt in each jar.
4. Wipe the rims of the jar with a clean damp towel, and then place the lids and the rings. Transfer the jars to the pressure canner and process them at 10 pounds pressure for 75 minutes.
5. Wait for the pressure canner to depressurize to zero before removing the jars using cooking tongs
6. Place the jars on a cooling rack for 24 hours to seal then store in a cool dry place.

Nutritional Information

Calories 182.6, Total fat 7.8g, Saturated fat 0.9g, Total carbs 1.0g, Net carbs 0.8g Protein 18.8g, Sugars 0g, Fiber 0.2g, Sodium 912.6mg, Potassium 24.9mg

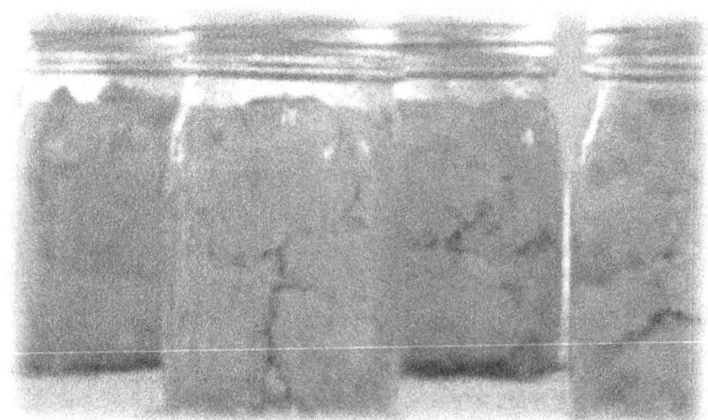

If you love store-bought canned chicken, this home-canned chicken breast will be rewarding to you. Not only does it save your money but also its canned with no preservatives added.
Prep time: 20 minutes, **Cook time:** 0 minutes, **Process time:** 75 minutes: **Serves** 5 pints

Ingredients

- 5 lb Chicken breast
- salt

Preparation Method

1. Cut the chicken into small pieces that will fit in the jars. Place the chicken in the sterilized jars leaving 1-inch headspace.
2. Add a 1/2 tablespoon of salt on each jar. You may add water but chicken makes its own juice.
3. Get lid of the air bubbles and wipe the jar rims with a damp cloth.
4. Put on the lids and the rings on the jars. Transfer the jars to the pressure canner and process them at 10 pounds pressure for 75 minutes.
5. Wait for the pressure canner to depressurize to zero before removing the jars.
6. Place the jars on a cooling rack for 24 hours then store in a cool dry place.

Nutritional Information

Calories 120, Total fat 2.5g, Saturated fat 1.3g, Total carbs 2.5g, Net carbs 2.5g Protein 25, Sugars 0g, Fiber 0g, Sodium 675mg, Potassium 0mg

Pressure Canned Turkey pieces

If you are a turkey lover and have plenty of turkey meat in your home, you can preserve some through the pressure canning. The meat comes out tasty and tender

Prep time: 3 hours, **Cook time:** 30 minutes, **Process time:** 75 minutes: **Serves** 5 pints

Ingredients

- 5 lb Turkey
- Boiling water

Preparation Method

1. Use a method of your choice to cook the turkey meat until it's 2/3 cooked.
2. Pack the turkey pieces in the sterilized jars then add water or stock leaving 1-inch headspace.
3. Remove the air bubbles and place and wipe the rims with a damp cloth.

4. Put on the lids and the rings on the jars. Transfer the jars to the pressure canner and process them at 10 pounds pressure for 65 minutes if the turkey had bones and for 75 minutes if without bones

5. Wait for the pressure canner to depressurize to zero before removing the jars.

6. Place the jars on a cooling rack for 24 hours then store in a cool dry place.

Nutritional Information

Calories 262, Total fat 10.1g, Saturated fat 1.3g, Total carbs 40g, Net carbs 2.5g Protein 25, Sugars 0g, Fiber 0g, Sodium 111mg, Potassium 0mg

McDonald's Pressure Canned Fish

This is a simple seafood canning recipe that will amaze you. The canned fish tastes soo good that you will want to can and eat it more and more

Prep time: 20 minutes, **Cook time:** 0 minutes, **Process time:** 100 minutes: **Serves** 10 pints

Ingredients

- 20 11" blue backs
- Onions
- 2 tbsp pickling salt
- 9 tbsp white vinegar
- 9 tbsp ketchup

Preparation Method

1. Clean the fish, remove the skin, and cut it into 2 chunks.

2. In a small bowl, mix salt vinegar and ketchup.

3. Now layer the ingredients in the sterilized jars such that you start with fish, onions, and a tablespoon of the vinegar mixture. Repeat with all the jars leaving a headspace of 1/4 inch.

4. Wipe the rims and place the lids and the rings on the jars.

5. Place the jars in the pressure canner and process them at 11 lb for 100 minutes.

6. Wait for the pressure canner to depressurize to zero before removing the jars.

7. Place the jars on a cooling rack for 24 hours then store in a cool dry place.

Calories 138, Total fat 4g, Saturated fat 0.2g, Total carbs 0g, Net carbs 0g Protein 25, Sugars 0g, Fiber 0g, Sodium 560mg, Potassium 0mg

Pressure Canned Salmon

If you are a lover of salmon and have enough to eat and preserve, here is a recipe for you. The salmon comes out packed with salt flavor that makes it perfect.

Prep time: 20 minutes, **Cook time:** 0 minutes, **Process time:** 100 minutes: **Serves** 6 pints

Ingredients

- 5lb salmon
- salt

Preparation Method

1. Eviscerate the salmon immediately after catching it then clean it thoroughly with clean water.
2. Chill it until you are ready to pressure can it. Remove the tail, the head, and the fins. Split the fish lengthwise then cut into small pieces that perfectly fit in your jars.
3. Pack the fish in sterilized jars leaving a 1-inch headspace. Add a tablespoon of salt in each jar if you desire.
4. Wipe the jar rims with a damp paper towel then place the lids and the rings on the jar.
5. Process the jars in the pressure canner at 11 pounds pressure for 100 minutes.
6. Wait for the pressure canner to depressurize to zero before removing the jars.
7. Place the jars on a cooling rack for 24 hours then store in a cool dry place.

Nutritional Information

Calories 121, Total fat 5.4g, Saturated fat 1.3g, Total carbs 0g, Net carbs 0g Protein 17, Sugars 0g, Fiber 0g, Sodium 37.4mg, Potassium 0mg

Pressure Canned Tuna

Tuna can be pressure canned either raw or when precooked. Precooking the tuna, however, removes the oils that give it a strong flavor. It's perfect when pressure canned raw in its juices.

Prep time: 20 minutes, **Cook time:** 0 minutes, **Process time:** 100 minutes: **Serves** 6 pints

Ingredients

- 5 lb tuna
- salt

Preparation Method

1. Use a sharp kitchen knife to peel off the skin then scrape the surface to remove the blood vessels.
2. Cut the fish lengthwise, then into pieces that fit in a pint jar.
3. Add salt in each jar.
4. If you have precooked the tuna, add the fish, some vegetable oil, and a tablespoon of salt per pint jar.
5. Wipe the rims and place the lids and the rings on the jars. Process the jars at 10 pounds pressure for 100 minutes.
6. Wait for the pressure canner to depressurize to zero before removing the jars.
7. Place the jars on a cooling rack for 24 hours then store in a cool dry place.

Nutritional Information

Calories 191, Total fat 1.4g, Saturated fat 0.7g, Total carbs 0g, Net carbs 0g Protein 42, Sugars 0g, Fiber 0g, Sodium 83mg, Potassium 0mg

Pressure canned Whole clams

These clams are so delicious that you will want to add more and more of them in your pantry. Their own juices give them a melt-in-the-mouth taste that no one can resist.

Prep time: 20 minutes, **Cook time:** 10 minutes, **Process time:** 60 minutes: **Serves** 7 pints

Ingredients

- 5 lb Clam
- 3 tbsp salt
- 2 tbsp lemon juice

Preparation Method

1. Keep the clams cold in ice until you are ready to pressure can them.
2. Scrub the shells then stream them over water for 5 minutes. Open the clams and remove meat. Save the juices.
3. Add a gallon of water in a mixing bowl then add at most 3 tablespoons of salt. Wash the clam meat in the salted water.
4. Add water in a shallow saucepan then add lemon juice. Bring the water to boil. Add the clam meat and boil for 2 minutes.
5. Heat the reserved lam juices until boiling.
6. Drain the meat and pack it loosely in the jars leaving 1-inch headspace. Pour the hot lam juice over the meat then remove the bubbles.
7. You may add boiling water if you run out of the clam juice.
8. Wipe the rims and place the lids and the rings on the jars. Process the jars at 10 pounds pressure for 60 minutes
9. Wait for the pressure canner to depressurize to zero before removing the jars.
10. Place the jars on a cooling rack for 12-24 hours undisturbed then store in a cool dry place.

Nutritional Information

Calories 148, Total fat 2g, Saturated fat 0.3g, Total carbs 5.1g, Net carbs 5.1g Protein 25.5, Sugars 0g, Fiber 0g,

Pressure Canned Minced Clams

These minced clams will make a classic salad when topped with crispy celery, onions all over lettuce leaves.

Prep time: 20 minutes, **Cook time:** 0 minutes, **Process time:** 60 minutes: **Serves** 5 pints

Ingredients

- 5 lb Clam
- 3 tbsp salt
- 2 tbsp lemon juice

Preparation Method

1. Keep the clams cold in ice until you are ready to pressure can them.
2. Scrub the shells then stream them over water for 5 minutes. Open the clams and remove meat. Save the juices.
3. Add a gallon of water in a mixing bowl then add at most 3 tablespoon of salt. Wash the clam meat in the salted water.
4. Add water in a shallow saucepan then add lemon juice. Bring the water to boil. Add the clam meat and boil for 2 minutes.
5. Heat the reserved lam juices until boiling.
6. Drain the meat and add it to the grinder or a food processor.
7. Pack 3/4 cup of minced clams in a half-pint leaving a headspace of 1- inch. Add the clam juices maintaining the headspace.
8. Remove any air bubbles and add more clam juice if necessary. In case you run out of clam juice, add boiling water.
9. Wipe the rims and place the lids and the rings on the half-pint jars. Process the jars at 10 pounds pressure for 60 minutes
10. Wait for the pressure canner to depressurize to zero before removing the jars.
11. Place the jars on a cooling rack undisturbed then store in a cool dry place

Nutritional Information

Calories 148, Total fat 2g, Saturated fat 0.3g, Total carbs 5.1g, Net carbs 5.1g Protein 25.5, Sugars 0g, Fiber 0g,

These pressure canned shrimps are a perfect make-ahead appetizer idea that will baffle you and your family. All you need is to remove it from the jar and serve it with seasonings of choice.

Prep time: 20 minutes, **Cook time:** 0 minutes, **Process time:** 45 minutes:

Serves 10 pints

Ingredients

- 10 lb Shrimp
- 1/4 cup salt
- 1 cup vinegar

Preparation Method

1. Remove the heads immediately you catch shrimp then chill until ready to preserve them.
2. Wash the shrimps and drain them well.
3. Add a gallon of water in a pot then add salt and vinegar. Bring to boil then cook shrimp for 10 minutes.
4. Use a slotted spoon to remove the shrimp from cooking liquid then rinse it in cold water and drain . Peel the shrimp while packing it in the sterilized jars.
5. Add a gallon of water with 3 tablespoon salt and bring it to a boil. Add the brine to the jars and remove the air bubbles. Add more brine if necessary.
6. Wipe the jar rims with a cloth damped in vinegar. Place the lids and the rings.
7. Process the jars at 10 pounds pressure for 45 minutes
8. Wait for the pressure canner to depressurize to zero before removing the jars.
9. Place the jars on a cooling rack undisturbed then store in a cool dry place

Nutritional Information

Calories 100, Total fat 2g, Saturated fat 0.8g, Total carbs 1g, Net carbs 1g Protein 15g, Sugars 0g, Fiber 0g

Canned Oysters

These pressure canned oysters are a real treasure in your pantry. They come out so good that they make a perfect quick diner in those busy midweek evenings.

Prep time: 30 minutes, **Cook time:** 10 minutes, **Process time:** 75 minutes: **Serves** 6 pints

Ingredients

- 5 lb oysters
- Salt
- water

Preparation Method

1. Wash the oysters in clean water then heat them in an oven at 400F for 7 minutes to open.
2. Cool them in ice-cold water. Remove the meat, placing it in water containing salt.
3. Drain the meat and pack in the jars leaving a 1-inch headspace. Add 1/2 tablespoon of salt in each half-pint jar and add water maintaining the headspace.
4. Wipe the jar rims then place the lids and the rings.
5. Process the jars at 10 pounds pressure for 75 minutes.
6. Wait for the pressure canner to depressurize to zero before removing the jars from the canner
7. Place the jars on a cooling rack undisturbed then store in a cool dry place

Nutritional Information

Calories 68, Total fat 3g, Saturated fat 1.7g, Total carbs 0g, Net carbs 0g Protein 7, Sugars 0g, Fiber 0g, Sodium 87mg, Potassium 0mg

Easy Canned Antelope meat

Make easy meals with this canned antelope in soups, stews or sandwiches. The delicious canned meat can also be heated and eaten as is.

Prep time: 15 minutes, **Cook time:** 0 minutes, **Process time:** 75 minutes: **Serves** 6 pints

Ingredients

- 1 lb lean meat, cubed
- 1 tbsp minced garlic
- 1 tbsp salt
- 1/4 tbsp black pepper, ground
- 4 sliced onions
- 1 tbsp green bell pepper, minced

Preparation Method

1. Place the meat in a mixing bowl and sprinkle with garlic, salt, and pepper.
2. Place the meat mixture in

sterilized jars with the onions and bell peppers. Leave a headspace of 1/2 inch headspace.

3. Wipe the rim with a damp cloth and place the lids and the rings.
4. Place the jars in a pressure canner filled with water according to the manufacturer directions.
5. Fix the lid and bring the water to boil. Process the jars at 10 pounds pressure for 75 minutes.
6. Wait for the pressure canner to depressurize to zero before removing the jars from the canner
7. Place the jars on a cooling rack undisturbed then store in a cool dry place

Nutritional Information

Calories 128, Total fat 2.5g, Saturated fat 1.0g, Total carbs 1.7g, Net carbs 1.4g Protein 23.3, Sugars 1g, Fiber 0.3g, Sodium 610mg, Potassium 205mg

Pressure Canned Deer Meat

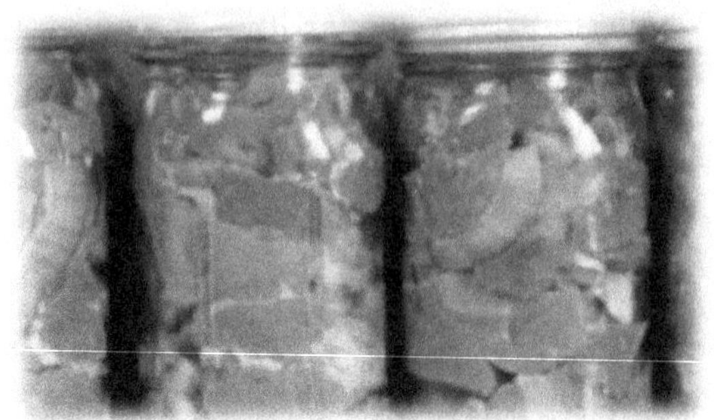

This canned deer meat makes the best stroganoff and barbecue ever. You can also use it for soups or in sandwiches too. So when traveling and come across a big deer, do not hesitate to bring it whole back home

Prep time: 15 minutes, **Cook time:** 0 minutes, **Process time:** 75 minutes: **Serves** 6 pints

Ingredients

*   20 lb Deer meat
*   Garlic
*   Non-ionized salt
*   Black pepper

Preparation Method

1. Trim the meat to remove as much fat and tendons as possible the cube the meat
2. Tightly pack the meat in jars then add 2garlic cloves, 1 tablespoon salt and 1/4 tablespoon pepper on top of the meat in each jar.
3. Wipe the jar rims and place the lids and the rings on the jars.

Place the jars in the pressure canner.

4. Process the jars at 15 pounds pressure for 90 minutes.
5. Wait for the pressure canner to depressurize to zero before removing the jars from the canner
6. Place the jars on a cooling rack undisturbed then store in a cool dry place

Calories 120, Total fat 2.4g, Saturated fat 1g, Total carbs 0g, Net carbs 0g Protein 23, Sugars 0g, Fiber 0g, Sodium 51mg, Potassium 0mg

Canned Beef Stroganoff

Yummy beef stroganoff in a can. It can be served over noodle base, over classic egg, or vegetables as a side dish

Prep time: 30 minutes, **Cook time:** 0 minutes, **Process time:** 75 minutes: **Serves** 4 pints

- 1 tbsp ground black pepper
- 2 tbsp salt
- 2 tbsp thyme, diced
- 2 tbsp parsley
- 4 tbsp tomato paste
- 4ntbsp Worcestershire sauce
- 2 garlic cloves
- 1 cup onion
- 1 cup mushrooms, sliced
- 2 lb stewing beef
- Hot beef broth

1. In a mixing bowl, mix pepper, salt, thyme, parsley, tomato paste, and Worcestershire.
2. Wash, peel, and slice the garlic cloves and onions, then wash and slice the mushrooms. Add to the mixing bowl.
3. Trim excess fat from the beef and cut into chunks. Add the meat to the bowl. Mix everything together until well combined.
4. Firmly pack the mixture in pint jars leaving a 1-inch headspace.
5. Wipe the rims and place the lids and rings on the jars.
6. Process the jars at 10-pound pressure for 75 minutes.

7. Wait for the pressure canner to depressurize to zero before removing the jars from the canner

8. Place the jars on a cooling rack undisturbed then store in a cool dry place

Calories 234, Total fat 6.3g, Saturated fat 2.3g, Total carbs 5.2g, Net carbs 4.3g Protein 37., Sugars 3.2g, Fiber 0-9g, Sodium 751mg, Potassium 643mg

Peggie's Pressure Canned Deer Meat

Peggie's canned deer meat is so good that you can eat it directly from the jars. Do not add liquids in the meat because the meat makes its own liquid.

Prep time: 20 minutes, **Cook time:** 0 minutes, **Process time:** 75 minutes: **Serves** 6 pints

- 2 chicken bouillon cubes
- 1-3/4 raw deer meat
- 1 tbsp canning salt
- 1 tbsp white vinegar

1. Place the meat in a pint jar leaving a 1-inch headspace
2. Heat the lids and place them on the jars.
3. Put 2 inches of tap water that is as hot as the jars in the pressure canner and place a regular lid on the canner.
4. Process the jars for 75 minutes at 10 pounds pressure

Calories 147, Total fat 2g, Saturated fat 1g, Total carbs 0g, Net carbs 0g Protein 27, Sugars 0g, Fiber 0g, Sodium 72mg, Potassium 0mg

CHAPTER 6: Soups, Stocks, broths, and stews

Canned Vegetable Soup

Are you a pressure canning fan? This pressure canned soup tastes amazing. It is a healthy recipe as tomatoes are a good source of potassium which is an essential mineral for heart disease prevention and blood pressure control. You will enjoy it.

Prep time: 5 minutes, **Cook time:** 30 minutes, **Process time:**85 minutes; **Serves** 7

Ingredients

- 8 cups chopped tomatoes, peeled and cored
- 6 cups cubed potatoes, peeled
- 6 cups carrots, 3/4 inch slices
- 4 cups green lima beans
- 4 cups corn kernels, uncooked
- 2 cups celery, 1-inch slices
- 2 cups onions, chopped
- 6 cups water

Optional: salt and pepper to taste

Preparation Method

1. Combine vegetables in a saucepot, large, and then add water.
2. Bring to boil for about 25 minutes on high then reduce heat to low and simmer for about 5 minutes.
3. Now season with pepper and salt if desired.
4. Scoop the hot soup into hot quart jars. Make sure you leave 1-inch headspace.
5. If needed, remove air bubbles adjusting headspace. Wipe the rims of the jars using a clean damp towel.
6. Place the lids and process quart jars in a pressure canner for about 85 minutes at 11 pounds pressure if using a dial-gauge canner or 10 pounds pressure if using a weighted-gauge canner.

Nutritional Information

Calories 354, Total fat 2.4g, Saturated fat 0.4g, Total carbs, 75.1g, Net carbs 59.7g, Protein 14.1g, Sugars 17.1g, Fiber 15.4g, Sodium 110mg, Potassium 2016mg

Pressure Canned Chicken Soup

This is truly and honestly the best way to preserve chicken soup. The soup is full of flavor, delicious, and perfect that all your family members will love.

Prep time: 10 minutes, **Cook time:** 1 hour, **Process time:** 90 minutes; **Serves** 4

Ingredients

- 16 cups chicken stock
- 1-1/2 cups celery, diced
- 3 cups chicken, diced
- 1 cup onion, diced
- 1-1/2 cups carrots, sliced

Optional: 3 chicken bouillon cubes

Optional: salt and pepper to taste

Preparation Method

1. Combine chicken stock, celery, chicken, onion, and carrots in a saucepot, large, and bring to boil on high for about 30 minutes.
2. Reduce heat to medium-low and simmer for about 30 minutes.
3. Add the optional ingredients and cook until bouillon cubes dissolve if desired.
4. Scoop the hot soup into hot quart jars and leave 1-inch headspace.
5. If needed, remove air bubbles adjusting headspace. Wipe the rims of the jars using a clean damp paper towel.
6. Now apply 2-piece metal caps.
7. Process quart jars in a pressure canner for 90 minutes at 11 pounds pressure if using a dial-gauge canner or 10 pounds pressure if using a weighted-gauge canner.

Nutritional Information

Calories 293, Total fat 5.7g, Saturated fat 1.5g, Total carbs 24.6g, Net carbs 18g, Protein 35.7g,

Sugars 13.4g, Fiber 6.6g, Sodium 3376mg, Potassium 1142mg

Canned Carrot and Ginger Soup

This pressure canned soup has a unique sweetness. It is also a healthy recipe as carrots are linked to a reduced risk of heart disease and improved eye health. Everyone will be left yearning for more.

Prep time: 5 minutes, **Cook time:** 1 hour, **Process time:** 85 minutes; **Serves** 7

Ingredients

- 3 tbsp butter
- 1 large peeled Spanish onion, diced
- 2 garlic cloves, whole and peeled
- 3 lbs peeled and sliced carrots
- 2 sliced ribs celery
- 3 tbsp fresh ginger, peeled and chopped
- 8 cups vegetable or chicken stock
- 1 tbsp coriander, ground
- 1/2 cup honey
- Salt and black pepper to taste

Preparation Method

1. Melt butter in a stockpot, stainless steel, over high-medium heat.
2. Add onion, garlic, carrots, celery, and ginger and sauté for about 10 minutes. Stir frequently.
3. Add stock and bring to boil. Reduce heat and simmer for 30-35 minutes until carrots are tender.
4. Remove from heat then add ginger, coriander, and honey.
5. Pour the soup into an immersion blender and blend until smooth.
6. Scoop the hot soup into sterilized jars and leave 1-inch headspace.
7. If needed, remove air bubbles adjusting headspace. Wipe the rims of the jars using a clean damp paper towel
8. Now apply 2-piece metal caps.
9. Process quart jars in a pressure canner for 85 minutes at 11 pounds pressure if using a dial-gauge canner or 10 pounds pressure if using a weighted-gauge canner.

Nutritional Information

Calories 224, Total fat 5.8g,
Saturated fat 3.3g, Total carbs 43.5g,
Net carbs 37.9g, Protein 3g, Sugars
31.1g, Fiber 5.6g, Sodium 1048mg,
Potassium 723mg

Pressure Canned Tomato Soup

This is one of the best pressure canned recipes to prepare in your home. This tomato soup may probably become your family's favorite soup and I bet everyone will enjoy it.

Prep time: 1 hour, **Cook time:** 15 minutes, **Process time:** 20 minutes; **Serves** 20

Ingredients

- 20lbs rinsed tomatoes, cut into small chunks
- 10 tbsp divided lemon juice

Preparation Method

1. Place tomatoes in a pot of boiling water then parboil the tomatoes for about 1-2 minutes until skins begin to come off.
2. Place a strainer into a large bowl.
3. Now remove and place the tomatoes on the strainer. Run them through a food mill to get rid of skins and seeds.
4. Transfer the puree into a stockpot over low heat and keep it warm until ready to pressure can.
5. Funnel lemon juice and warm tomato puree into canning jars. Leave 1-inch headspace.
6. If needed, remove air bubbles adjusting headspace. Wipe the rims of the jars using a clean damp paper towel.
7. Now apply 2-piece metal caps.
8. Process quart jars in a pressure canner for 15 minutes at 11 pounds pressure if using a dial-gauge canner or 10 pounds pressure if using a weighted-gauge canner.

Nutritional Information

Calories 83, Total fat 0g, Saturated 0g, Total 18g, Net carbs 13g, Protein 4g, Sugars 12g, Fiber 5g, Sodium 22mg, Potassium 1082mg

Canned Chicken Stock

This is a stock recipe that you and your family can have all week long without any complaining. It is a comforting, nourishing, and healthy pressure canned stock.

Prep time: 5 minutes, **Cook time:** 2 hours 20 minutes, **Process time:** 25 minutes; **Serves** 4

Ingredients

- 16 cups water
- 3-4 lbs chicken, pieces cut
- 2 stalks celery
- 2 quartered onions, medium
- 1 tbsp salt
- 10 peppercorns

Preparation Method

1. Prepare your pressure canner and heat your jars with simmering water. Wash the lids with soapy water, warm, and set the bands aside.
2. Place water and chicken in a saucepan, large, then bring to boil.
3. Reduce heat and simmer for about 2 hours until chicken becomes tender. Now remove from heat and skim off foam.
4. Remove and reserve the chicken for other use.
5. Meanwhile, strain the stock through several cheesecloth layers or a sieve and allow it to cool for fat to solidify. Now skim the fat off.
6. Heat to boiling the stock and scoop hot stock into hot pint jars. Leave 1-inch headspace.
7. Wipe the rims of the jars using a clean damp paper towel.
8. Center lid on jars then apply band adjusting until fingertip tight fit.
9. Process pint jars in a pressure canner for 20 minutes at 11 pounds pressure if using a dial-gauge canner or 10 pounds pressure if using a weighted-gauge canner.

Nutritional Information

Calories 709, Total fat 13.8g, Saturated fat 3.9g, Total carbs 5.6g, Net carbs 4.2g, Protein 132.2g, Sugars 2.4g, Fiber 1.4g, Sodium 2067mg, Potassium 964mg

American Chicken Stock

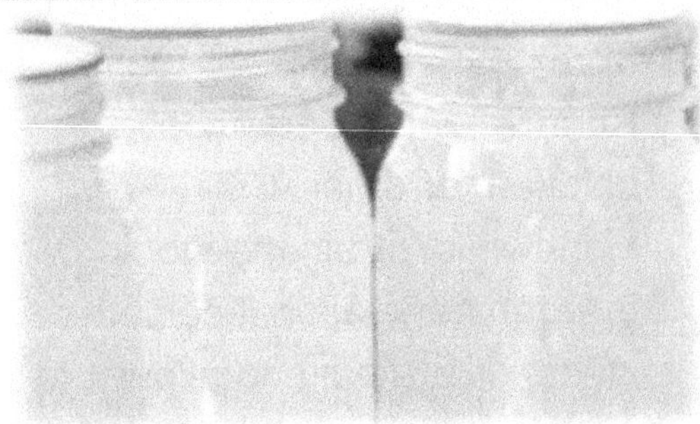

Looking for a super delicious stock? American chicken stock is the recipe you are looking for as it is delicious each and every time.

Prep time: 1 hour, **Cook time:** 25 minutes, **Process time:** 25 minutes; **Serves** 1

Ingredients

- Chicken bones, meat removed
- Water to cover

Preparation Method

1. Place bones in a pressure cooker and add water to cover
2. Cook on high pressure for about 30 minutes until the remaining meat falls off from the bones.
3. Strain the stock into a bowl, large, then discard loosened meat from bones. Refrigerate the stock overnight.
4. Skim off and discard fat then reheat the stock in a saucepot.
5. Pour the stock into 1-liter US quart jars leaving 1-inch headspace. Wipe the rims of the jars using a paper towel, dampened clean.
6. Apply 2-piece metal caps.
7. Process quart jars in a pressure canner for 25 minutes at 11 pounds pressure if using a dial-gauge canner or 10 pounds pressure if using a weighted-gauge canner.

Nutritional Information

Calories 17, Total fat 0g, Saturated fat 0g, Total carbs 2g, Net carbs 2g, Protein 2g, Sugar 2g, Fiber 0g, Sodium 67mg, Potassium 167mg

Home-canned Beef Stock

This makes a healthy beef stock by pressure canning. Pressure canned beef stock is the best option for

preparing stock for your family. Beef makes the stock delicious.

Prep time: 10 minutes, **Cook time:** 2-4 hours, **Process time:** 20 minutes; **Serves** 4

Ingredients

- 4 lbs meaty beef bones
- 1 finely chopped onion, medium
- 1 sliced large carrot
- 1 sliced stalk celery
- 1 bay leaf, medium
- Salt to taste
- 3 parsley sprigs, fresh
- 3 whole peppercorns
- 1 whole garlic clove
- 1/2 tbsp thyme, dried
- 2 quarts water

Preparation Method

1. Optional: place bones on a roasting pan, large, and bake for about 30 minutes. Add vegetables then bake for another 30 minutes until evenly browned bones. Turn occasionally.
2. Transfer vegetables and bones into a stockpot, scrape the roasting pan with 2 cups water then add to the stockpot.
3. Add remaining water and boil on high heat. Reduce heat to low-medium skimming off foam.
4. Add bay leaf, cover, and simmer for about 2-4 hours.
5. Remove and discard bones then strain the stock through a sieve, fine.
6. Discard bay leaf and vegetables, cool, and skim off fat. It's recommended refrigerating overnight.
7. Now bring the stock to boiling and scoop hot stock into hot pint jars. Leave 1-inch headspace.
8. Wipe the jar rims using a clean damp paper towel then apply 2-piece metal caps.
9. Process quart jars in a pressure canner for 20 minutes at 11 pounds pressure if using a dial-gauge canner or 10 pounds pressure if using a weighted-gauge canner.

Nutritional Information

Calories 388, Total fat 28.4g, Saturated fat 11.1g, Total carbs 5.4g, Net carbs 4g, Protein 26.5g, Sugars 2.2g, Fiber 1.4g, Sodium 148mg, Potassium 439mg

Canned Turkey stock

Do you need to impress your family? It is a perfect and excellent stock recipe that is pressure canned and it is a healthy recipe. You will love it. **Prep time:** 1 hour, **Cook time:** 25 minutes, **Process time:** 25 minutes; **Serves** 1

Ingredients

- Turkey bones, meat removed
- Water to cover
- optional: salt to taste
- 1 bay leaf

Preparation Method

1. Place bones and water to cover the bones in a pressure cooker.
2. Add bay leaf and cook on high pressure for about 30 minutes until the remaining meat falls off from the bones.
3. Strain the stock into a bowl, large, and then discard loosened meat from bones. Refrigerate the stock overnight.
4. Skim off and discard fat then reheat the stock in a saucepot.
5. Pour the stock into quart jars leaving 1-inch headspace. Wipe the rims of the jars using a clean damp paper towel.
6. Apply 2-piece metal caps.
7. Process quart jars in a pressure canner for 25 minutes at 11 pounds pressure if using a dial-gauge canner or 10 pounds pressure if using a weighted-gauge canner.

Nutritional Information

Calories 20, Total fat 0g, Saturated fat 0g, Total carbs 1g, Net carbs 1g, Protein 4g, Sugars 1g, Fiber 0g, Sodium 130mg, Potassium 252mg

Pressure Canned Turkey Broth

This is a fancy way to prepare and serve turkey broth impressing all your guests and your kids. This pressure canned turkey broth is a recipe that everyone might be left yearning for more

Prep time: 10 minutes, **Cook time:** 30-45 minutes, **Process time:** 25 minutes; **Serves** 2

Ingredients

- Turkey carcass bones, meat removed
- Optional: 2 quartered onions
- Optional: 2 sliced celery stalks
- Optional: 2 bay leaves
- Optional: Salt to taste
- Water to cover

Preparation Method

1. Place turkey bones and all optional ingredients in a stockpot, large, then add water to cover everything.
2. Cover the pot and simmer for about 30-45 minutes until remaining meat tidbits fall off easily.
3. Remove and discard bones then strain the broth and discard bay leaves and vegetables.
4. Cool the broth then skim off the fat and discard it. Season with salt if desired.
5. Reheat your broth to boiling.
6. Scoop broth into quart jars. Leave 1-inch headspace.
7. Wipe the jar rims using a clean damp paper towel, and then apply 2-piece metal caps.
8. Process quart jars in a pressure canner for 25 minutes at 11 pounds pressure if using a dial-gauge canner or 10 pounds pressure if using a weighted-gauge canner.

Nutritional Information

Calories 233, Total fat 13.1g, Saturated fat 3.8g, Total carbs 12.1g, Net carbs 9g, Protein 16.5g, Sugars 4.9g, Fiber 3.1g, Sodium 171mg, 18mg

This recipe is easy, delicious, and quick to cook. Beef broth is a perfect recipe for someone who hates chaos or rushing to get meals ready. Pressure-can beef broth and you won't regret.

Prep time: 15 minutes, **Cook time:** 3-4 hours, **Process time:** 25 minutes; **Serves** 4

Ingredients

- Beef bones, trimmed and meat removed
- Optional: 2 quartered onions
- Optional: 2 sliced carrots
- Optional: 2 sliced celery stalks
- Optional: 2 bay leaves
- salt to taste
- Water to cover

Preparation Method

1. Prepare the bones by cracking them to enhance flavor extraction. Now rinse them.
2. Now place the bones and optional ingredients if using in a stockpot, large.
3. Add water to cover everything then cover the pot. Simmer for about 3-4 hours.
4. Remove and discard bones, vegetables, and bay leaves. Now cool the broth, skim off the fat and discard it.
5. If desired, season with salt.
6. Reheat your broth to boiling.
7. Scoop the hot broth into hot quart jars leaving 1-inch headspace.
8. Wipe the jar rims using a clean and damp paper towel, and then apply 2-piece metal caps.
9. Process quart jars in a pressure canner for 25 minutes at 11 pounds pressure if using a dial-gauge canner or 10 pounds pressure if using a weighted-gauge canner.

Nutritional Information

Calories 207, Total fat 7.8g, Saturated fat 2.9g, Total carbs 9.1g, Net carbs 6.8g, Protein 24.3g, Sugars 3.9g, Fiber 2.3g, Sodium 101mg, Potassium 486mg

Pressure Canned Chicken Broth

This chicken broth is fast, easy to make, juicy, and delicious. It is a recipe that is best prepare by pressure canning and which will make you feel confident using a pressure canner.

Prep time: 10 minutes, **Cook time:** 30-45 minutes, **Process time:** 25 minutes; **Serves** 2

- Chicken carcass bones, meat removed
- Optional: 2 quartered onions
- Optional: 2 sliced celery stalks
- Optional: 2 bay leaves
- Optional: Salt to taste
- Water to cover

Preparation Method

1. Place chicken bones and all optional ingredients in a stockpot, large, then add water to cover everything.
2. Cover the pot and simmer for about 30-45 minutes until remaining meat tidbits fall off easily.
3. Remove and discard bones then strain the broth and discard bay leaves and vegetables.
4. Cool the broth then skim off the fat and discard it. Season with salt if desired.
5. Reheat your broth to boiling.
6. Scoop broth into quart jars. Leave 1-inch headspace.
7. Wipe the jar rims using a clean damp paper towel, then apply 2-piece metal caps.
8. Process quart jars in a pressure canner for 25 minutes at 11 pounds pressure if using a dial-gauge canner or 10 pounds pressure if using a weighted-gauge canner.

Nutritional Information

Calories 233, Total fat 13.1g, Saturated fat 3.8g, Total carbs 12.1g, Net carbs 9g, Protein 16.5g, Sugars 4.9g, Fiber 3.1g, Sodium 171mg, 18mg

Pressure Canned Beef Stew

Are you looking for an anytime stew recipe to always impress your guests? Pressure canned beef stew is the one for you as it is delicious and will leave everyone asking for more.

Prep time: 5 minutes, **Cook time:** 30 minutes, **Process time:** 90 minutes; **Serves** 7

Ingredients

- 4-5lbs beef stew meat, 1-1/2-inch cubes

- 1 tbsp vegetable oil
- 12 cups potatoes, peeled and cubed
- 8 cups carrots, sliced
- 3 cups celery, chopped
- 3 cups onion, chopped
- 1-1/2 tbsp salt
- 1 tbsp thyme
- 1/2 tbsp pepper
- Water to cover

1. Brown meat in a saucepot, large, in oil.
2. Add vegetables and all seasonings then cover with water. Boil the stew and remove it from heat.
3. Scoop the hot stew into hot quart jars. Leave 1-inch headspace.
4. If needed, remove air bubbles adjusting headspace. Wipe the rims of the jars using a paper towel, dampened clean.
5. Now apply 2-piece metal caps.
6. Process quart jars in a pressure canner for about 90 minutes at 11 pounds pressure if using a dial-gauge canner or 10 pounds pressure if using a weighted-gauge canner.

Calories 877, Total fat 22.6g, Saturated fat 8.1g, Total carbs 59.2g, Net carbs 47.9g, Protein 104.6g, Sugars 11.8g, Fiber 11.3g, Sodium 5839mg, Potassium 2950mg

Canned Hearty Chili Stew

This is a delicious and a perfect recipe to prepare in a pressure canner. Hearty chili stew is healthy as chilis are linked in the promotion of weight loss.

Prep time: 10 minutes, **Cook time:** 1 hour, **Process time:** 90 minutes; **Serves** 6

- 4 lbs beef chunk, boneless, fat removed and 1/2-inch cubes
- 1/4 cup vegetable oil
- 3 cups onion, diced
- 2 minced garlic cloves
- 5 tbsp chili powder

- 2 tbsp cumin seed
- 2 tbsp salt
- 1 tbsp oregano
- 1/2 tbsp pepper
- 1/2 tbsp coriander
- 1/2 tbsp red pepper, crushed
- 6 cups canned tomatoes, diced and undrained

Preparation Method

1. Brown meat cubes in hot oil lightly then add garlic and onions. Cook until soft and not brown.
2. Add all the remaining spices and cook for about 5 minutes.
3. Add tomatoes and stir then bring to boil on high.
4. Reduce medium-low heat and simmer for about 45-60 minutes. Stir occasionally.
5. Scoop hot chili stew into hot pint jars. Leave 1-ich headspace.
6. If needed, remove air bubbles adjusting headspace. Wipe the rims of the jars using a paper towel, dampened clean.
7. Now apply 2-piece metal caps.
8. Process pint jars in a pressure canner for about 90 minutes at 11 pounds pressure if using a dial-gauge canner or 10 pounds pressure if using a weighted-gauge canner.

Nutritional Information

Calories 733, Total fat 30g, Saturated fat 9.2g, Total carbs 18.6g, Net carbs 12.2g, Protein 95.6g, Sugars 8.2g, Fiber 6.4g, Sodium 2603mg, Potassium 1927mg

Canned Chili Corn Carne

Chili corn carne comes with a very wonderful taste when prepared in a pressure canner. It is a delicious stew that you can have any time. **Prep time:** 20 minutes, **Cook time:** 1 hour, **Process time:** 75 minutes; **Serves** 9

Ingredients

- 3 cups pinto bean or red kidney beans, dried and washed
- 5-1/2 cups water
- 5 tbsp salt, divided
- 3 lbs ground beef
- 1-1/2 cups onion, chopped
- 1 cup pepper, chopped

- 1 tbsp black pepper
- 3-6 tbsp chili powder
- 8 cups tomatoes, crushed or whole

Preparation Method

1. Place beans in a saucepan, 2-quart, then add cold water to 2-3 inches above beans. Cover and refrigerate for about 12-18 hours to soak. Now drain the beans and discard water.
2. Place the beans in a saucepot with 5-1/2 cups water. Season with 2 tbsp salt and bring to boil for about 25 minutes.
3. Reduce heat to low and simmer for about 30 minutes.
4. Meanwhile, brown beef with onions and pepper (optional) in a skillet then drain the fat off.
5. Add 3 tbsp salt, and the remaining ingredients together with cooked beans and simmer for about 5 minutes. Make sure not to thicken.
6. Scoop hot chili stew into hot pint jars. Leave 1-inch headspace. Do not use quart jars.
7. If needed, remove air bubbles adjusting headspace. Wipe the rims of the jars using a clean damp paper towel
8. Now apply 2-piece metal caps.
9. Process pint jars in a pressure canner for about 75 minutes at 11 pounds pressure if using a dial-gauge canner or 10 pounds pressure if using a weighted-gauge canner.

Nutritional Information

Calories 556, Total fat 11.4g, Saturated fat 3.9g, Total carbs 51g, Net carbs 37g, Protein 61.9g, Sugars 6.7g, Fiber 14g, Sodium 4062mg, Potassium 2016mg

Venison Stew with Veggies

This may probably become your favorite pressure canned stew. This venison stew with veggies is an addictive and ultimately delicious recipe that everyone will love.

Prep time: 10 minutes, **Cook time:** 30 minutes, **Process time:** 1 hour 30 minutes; **Serves** 7

Ingredients

- 1 tbsp olive oil
- 4-5 lbs trimmed venison stew meat, 1-inch cubes
- 3 qts potatoes, 1-inch cubes
- 2 qts carrots, largely diced
- 3 cups celery, chopped
- Optional: 1-1/2 tbsp salt
- 1 tbsp thyme, dried
- 1/2 - 1 tsp black pepper
- **Optional:** Garlic cloves
- Water to cover

Preparation Method

1. Put oil in a stockpot, large, and brown meat cubes.
2. Add veggies and all seasoning leaving out the thyme and garlic cloves for later use.
3. Pour water, boiling, to cover the mixture. Boil the mixture fully.
4. Now place thyme and cloves directly into quart jars.
5. Scoop hot venison stew into hot quart jars. Leave 1-inch headspace.
6. If needed, remove air bubbles adjusting headspace. Wipe the rims of the jars using a clean damp towel
7. Now apply 2-piece metal caps.
8. Process pint jars in a pressure canner for about 1 hour 30 minutes at 11 pounds pressure if using a dial-gauge canner or 10 pounds pressure if using a weighted-gauge canner.

Nutritional Information

Calories 260, Total fat 4.5g, Saturated fat 1g, Total carbs 25g, Net carbs 22g, Protein 30g, Sugars 4g, Fiber 3g, Sodium 260mg, Potassium 674mg

CHAPTER 7: Meals in Jar

Canned Chicken in jars

This is a flavorful healthy pressure canned recipe that is great to have for lunch or dinner. Chicken in jars is addictive and seriously delicious.
Prep time: 30 minutes, **Cook time:** 0 minutes, **Process time:** 90minutes; **Serves** 2

Ingredients

- 1 lb chicken
- 1/2 tbsp salt

Preparation Method

1. Slice the chicken and place it into quart jars leaving 1-inch headspace.
2. Put salt into the jars.
3. Wipe the rims of the jars using a clean damp towel.
4. Now apply 2-piece metal caps.
5. Process pint jars in a pressure canner for about 90 minutes at 11 pounds pressure if using a dial-gauge canner or 10 pounds pressure if using a weighted-gauge can.

Nutritional Information

Calories 342, Total fat 6.9g, Saturated fat 1.9g, Total carbs 0g, Net carbs 0g, Protein 65.7g, Sugars 0g, Fiber 0g, Sodium 1887mg, Potassium 424mg

Corned Beef and Potatoes

Canning corned beef creates an

instant, a shelf-stable item, and a healthier fast food. This is a hearty meal consisting of potatoes and corned beef brisket.

Prep time: 20 minutes, **Cook time:** 30 minutes, **Process time:** 85 minutes; **Serves** 8

- 8 cups water
- 1 tbsp pickling spice blend
- 4-5 lbs home-cured brisket, fat removed and 1-inch cubes
- 8-10 cups peeled Russet potatoes, 1-inch cubes

1. Boil water in a kettle.
2. In the meantime, place 1/4 tbsp of spice blend into each quart jar.
3. Layer brisket and potatoes into the jars. Leave 1-inch headspace.
4. Fill the jars with boiled water. Leave 1-inch headspace.
5. Remove air bubbles adjusting headspace. Wipe the rims of the jars using a clean damp towel.
6. Now apply 2-piece metal caps.
7. Process pint jars in a pressure canner for about 85 minutes at 11 pounds pressure if using a dial-gauge canner or 10 pounds pressure if using a weighted-gauge canner.

Calories, 465, Total fat 15.9g, Saturated fat 6g, Total carbs 0g, Net carbs 0g, Protein 99.4g, Sugars 0g, Fiber 0g, Sodium 433mg, Potassium 608mg

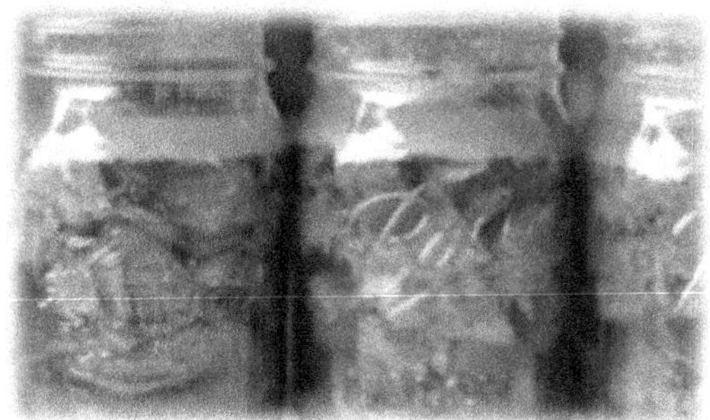

Canned Hungarian Goulash

Hungarian goulash is an easy recipe to make and get canned. Using a pressure canner this goulash might become your favorite canned meal to have in a jar.

Prep time: 10 minutes, **Cook time:** 30 minutes, **Process time:** 90 minutes; **Serves** 10

- 4 tbsp Hungarian paprika
- Pepper and salt to taste
- 2 tbsp mustard, dry
- 1 tbsp olive oil

- 4 quartered onions
- 4 minced garlic cloves
- 4 lb beef
- 4 coins sliced carrots
- 6 diced potatoes
- 2 diced bell peppers
- 6 cups Water
- 1/2 cup red wine vinegar
- 1 can tomato paste

Preparation Method

1. Mix Hungarian paprika, pepper, salt, and mustard in a bowl.
2. Heat oil in a stockpot, large, and sauté onions and garlic.
3. Deep beef into the spice mixture then transfers into the stockpot to brown lightly.
4. Layer beef, carrots, potatoes, and peppers into quart jars.
5. Now add water, vinegar, and tomato paste to the stockpot. Mix together with spices and boil the mixture.
6. Scoop the liquid into jars with layered contents removing any air bubbles in the jars. Leave 1-inch headspace.
7. Lid the jars then place them in a pressure canner.
8. Process for about 90 minutes at 10 pounds pressure on altitude basis.

Nutritional Information

Calories 509, Total fat 14g, Saturated fat 4.6g, Total carbs 34.4g, Net carbs 27.4g, Protein 59.9g, Sugars 8.3g, Fiber 7g, Sodium 169mg, Potassium 1705mg

Pressure canned Garlic Beef Stroganoff

Do you love beef ? This is the best beef recipe for you. Pressure canning beef stroganoff is easy and everyone will love it as beef has flavor and is delicious.

Prep time: 10 minutes, **Cook time:** 30 minutes, **Process time:** 90 minutes; **Serves** 10

Ingredients

- 1 tbsp butter
- 3-4 pounds beef
- 4 finely chopped garlic cloves
- 2 finely chopped onions
- 4 cups sliced mushrooms
- 2 tbsp Worcestershire sauce

- 4 cups Water
- Pepper and salt to taste

Preparation Method

1. Place butter in a stockpot and sauté beef, garlic, onions, and mushrooms until browned lightly.
2. Stir in sauce and water. This is to deglaze your stockpot. Scrape the stockpot bottom to loosen flavorful pieces.
3. Add 1 cup water, stir, and bring to a boil.
4. Scoop stroganoff into sterilized jars, making sure sauce is evenly distributed.
5. Lid the jars then place them in a pressure canner.
6. Process for about 90 minutes at 10 pounds pressure.

Nutritional Information

Calories 367, Total fat 12.6g, Saturated fat 5g, Total carbs 4g, Net carbs 3.2g, Protein 56.3g, Sugars 2g, Fiber 0.8g, Sodium 182mg, Potassium 858mg

Pressure Canned Chicken Cacciatore

Oh yes! Canning chicken cacciatore is irresistible and is next-level good. This is an amazing recipe and makes a perfect dinner dish. You will love it.

Prep time: 20 minutes, **Cook time:** 0 minutes, **Process time:** 90 minutes; **Serves** 4

Ingredients

- 3 lbs boneless chicken, bite-size pieces
- 2 cups sliced mushrooms
- 4 garlic cloves
- 2 cups green and red peppers, chunks cut
- 2 cups onions, 8ths cut
- 1 bottle red wine
- 2 tbsp oregano
- 2 tbsp basil
- 2 tbsp thyme
- 4 cups tomatoes, diced and with juices
- Salt to taste
- Pepper to taste

Preparation Method

1. Layer chicken, mushrooms, garlic, peppers, and onions in quart jars.
2. Boil wine, herbs and tomatoes in a stockpot, large. Scoop the hot liquid over layered ingredients in the jars.
3. Lid the jars then place them in a pressure canner.
4. Process for about 90 minutes at 10 pounds pressure on an altitude basis.

Nutritional Information

Calories 788, Total fat 11.8g, Saturated fat 3.2g, Total carbs 34.1g, Net carbs 23.7g, Protein 104.7g, Sugars 9.4g, Fiber 10.4g, Sodium 285mg, Potassium 1739mg

Canned Tamales

Looking for a crowd-pleaser? Canned tamales is the recipe for you as it comes out great and everyone one will love. This recipe will wake up taste buds.

Prep time: 30 minutes, **Cook time:** 10 minutes, **Process time:** 60 minutes; **Serves** 45

Ingredients

Meat filling
- 3 lb ground beef
- 1 chopped onion
- 3 tbsp minced garlic
- 3 tbsp salt

To add to meat after grinding
- 5 tbsp chili powder
- 1 tbsp salt
- 2 cups water
- 1/2 tbsp cayenne pepper, ground
- 2 tbsp all-purpose flour

Cornmeal spread
- 4-1/2 cups extra-fine cornmeal
- 1 tbsp salt
- 2 tbsp chili powder
- 5 cups water

Preparation Method

1. Brown beef draining off fat. Add onion, salt and garlic then mix well.
2. Place the mixture through a food grinder with the finest blade.
3. Add the ingredients for after grinding and simmer until thick over medium heat for about 5 minutes.
4. Meanwhile, mix together

cornmeal spread ingredients until smooth. Now spread 1/4 - inch thick of the mixture on 6x3" parchment paper strips. Leave enough space for turning over.

5. Spread 2 tbsp of the meat mixture through the meal dough center. Now roll up and fold sides and ends of the parchment paper.
6. Pack the tamales into clean pint jars, about 6-7 tamales in a single jar.
7. Add 1 tbsp water to each jar and put lids and bands on screwing them firmly tight down.
8. Process in a pressure canner for about 60 minutes at 10 pounds of pressure.

Nutritional Information

Calories 111, Total fat 2.5g, Saturated fat 0.7g, Total carbs 12.1g, Net carbs 10.4g, Protein 10.6g, Sugars 0.2g, Fiber 1.7g, Sodium 808mg, Potassium 192mg

Hamburger Sauce Mix

This recipe is a mixture of meat that you can use as base for several dishes such as tacos, spaghetti sauce, chili, or sloppy joes. The recipes can just be great for any meal.

Prep time: 20 minutes, **Cook time:** 20 minutes, **Process time:** 75 minutes; **Serves** 4

Ingredients

- 2 lbs lean beef, ground
- 3 cups chopped onions
- 2, 6 oz, cans tomato puree
- 1-1/3 cups water
- 1/2 tbsp pepper

Preparation Method

1. Brown beef and onions in a stockpot and skim off fat.
2. Add all the remaining ingredients and boil. Reduce heat and simmer for about 5 minutes.

3. Scoop the hot mixture into hot pint jars. Leave 1-inch headspace.
4. Wipe the rims of the jars using a clean damp paper towel and apply 2-piece metal caps.
5. Place the jars in a pressure canner and process for about 75 minutes at 10 pounds of pressure.

Nutritional Information

Calories 490, Total fat 14.4g, Saturated fat 5.4g, Total carbs 16.2g, Net carbs 12.5g, Protein 71.2g, Sugars 7.8g, Fiber 3.7g, Sodium 183mg, Potassium 1425mg

Pressure Canned spicy corn

Sometimes we all need a healthy meal that will take away all our hunger and this canned corn satisfies all that. It is a meal that might become one of your favorites.

Prep time: 30 minutes, **Cook time:** 55-75 minutes, **Process time:** 1 hour 25 minutes; **Serves** 40

Ingredients

- 32 pounds corn on the cob
- 2 garlic cloves
- 1 tbsp salt
- pepper
- 3-1/2 cups water

Preparation Method

1. Remove silk and husk from the corn then cut kernels from cob.
2. Fill quart jars with corn. Leave 1-inch headspace.
3. Season with garlic, salt and pepper to taste then add boiling water to cover the corns. Release trapped air bubbles by jiggling the jars.
4. Add 1 tbsp salt on each jar.
5. Wipe the rims of the jars using a paper towel, dampened clean and place on the lid and ring securely.
6. Place the jars in a pressure canner and process for about 1 hour 25 minutes at 10 pounds of pressure.

Nutritional Information

Calories 337, Total fat 2.7g, Saturated fat 0.4g, Total carbs 81g,

Net carbs 70.8g, Protein 11.3g,
Sugars 13g, Fiber 10.2g, Sodium
192mg, Potassium 912mg

Basic Pork and Beans

Pork and beans is a delicious and flavorful meal prepared in a pressure canner. It is a healthy recipe as pork is a rich source of protein which is effective for maintenance and growth of muscle mass.

Prep time: 2 hours, **Cook time:** 30 minutes, **Process time:** 75 minutes; **Serves** 8

Ingredients

- 3 lbs beans, dried, rinsed and sorted
- 6 cups Water
- 1-2 lbs pork
- Salt to taste
- 6 small onions, halved
- 12 bay leaves

Preparation Method

1. Soak beans in hot water for about 2 hours or overnight. Discard water.
2. Add fresh water to the beans and bring to boil. Drain the beans and reserve the water.
3. Distribute pork into pint jars evenly then top with beans leaving 1-inch headspace.
4. Add 2 bay leaves, an onion, and a pinch of salt to each jar.
5. Meanwhile, boil 6 cups of the reserved liquid.
6. Scoop the hot liquid into the jars and leave 1-inch headspace but totally covering the beans.
7. Lid the jars and place them in a pressure canner.
8. Process for about 75 minutes at 10 pounds of pressure while adjusting for altitude.

Nutritional Information

Calories 256, Total fat 4.5g, Saturated fat 1.5g, Total carbs 21.9g, Net carbs 13.6g, Protein 33.9g, Sugars 5.9g, Fiber 8.3g, Sodium 103mg, Potassium 969mg

Canned Dry Kidney beans

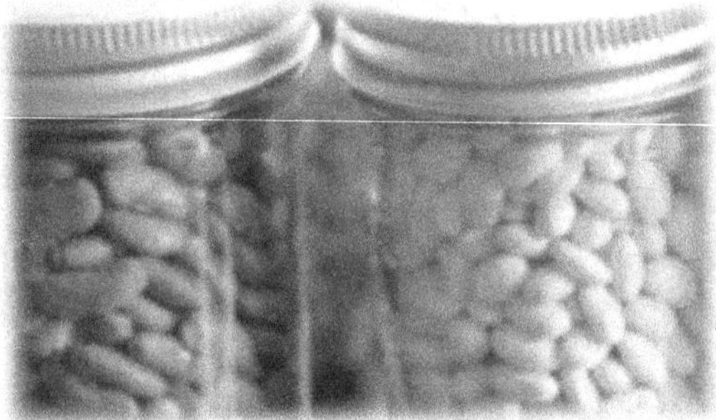

Looking for a quick and a satisfying canned weeknight supper? This is a perfect recipe for you as it is also healthy. Beans bring protein and fiber to your meal.

Prep time: 2 hours, **Cook time:** 45 minutes, **Process time:** 1 hour 30 minutes; **Serves** 8

Ingredients

- 3 lbs black beans, dried
- Water
- 2 tbsp vinegar

Preparation Method

1. Sort the beans to remove any foreign objects.
2. Place the beans in a bowl and cover with water. Add vinegar and soak for about 2 hours or overnight.
3. Drain the beans then rinse and place in a large pot. Cover with 2-inch water, fresh, and boil.
4. Scoop the beans into hot jars and leave 1-inch headspace.
5. Fill the jars with cooking liquid. Leave 1-inch headspace.
6. Put on lids and rings to the jars and place them in a pressure canner.
7. Process for about 1 hour 30 minutes at 10 pounds of pressure.
8. Remove jars from the canner and cool. Check lids if they are properly sealed then store.

Nutritional Information

Calories 581, Total fat 2.4g, Saturated fat 0.6g, Total carbs 106.1g, Net carbs 80.2g, Protein 36.7g, Sugars 3.6g, Fiber 25.9g, Sodium 12mg, Potassium 2527mg

Canned Pickled Small Beets

There is nothing great like delicious beets in the depths of cold winter. Conned pickled beets is a great recipe that makes pickling easier than you think. You will enjoy it.
Prep time: 30 minutes, **Cook time:** 35 minutes, **Process time: 35** minutes; **Serves** 4

Ingredients

- 4-5 lbs small beets
- 2 tbsp pickling salt
- 1-1/2 cups white sugar
- 3 cups white vinegar
- 2 tbsp pickling spice, mixed and tied in cheesecloth bag
- 1 cup water

Preparation Method

1. Wash and remove most beets tops. Leave 1/2 -inch beet top.
2. Cook the beets in a boiling pot of water, large; until barely tender then remove from heat.
3. Submerge cooked beets in a bowl, large, of ice water for the skin to come off easily.
4. Completely cut off tops and roots of the beets then remove the skin. Slice into large chunks.
5. Meanwhile, combine the remaining ingredients in a pot, non-reactive, and boil the mixture. Reduce heat to low and simmer for about 10 minutes.
6. Add beets to the liquid mixture and boil again. Remove the pickling spice bag.
7. Ladle beets and pickling liquid carefully into hot pint jars, sterilized. Leave 1/2 -inch headspace.
8. Use a non-metal utensil to remove air bubbles, if any, and add more pickling if needed but still maintain a proper headspace.
9. Wipe the pint jar rims using a damp cloth, clean, for proper sealing.

10. Seal the jars and process in a pressure canner for about 35 minutes.
11. For altitudes exceeding 3000ft (914m), add processing time by 5 minutes.

Nutritional Information

Calories 527, Total fat 1g, Saturated fat 0g, Total carbs 120g, Net carbs 107g, Protein 7g, Sugars 105g, Fiber 13g, Sodium 3852mg, Potassium 1505mg

Pickled Pullet Eggs

Are you a beginner in pressure canning? Pickled pullet eggs are a dish that you will enjoy preparing. It is a recipe that you can surprise your family with and they will absolutely love it. Thanks to this recipe.

Prep time: 30 minutes, **Cook time:** 20 minutes, **Process time:** 15 minutes; **Serves** 20

Ingredients

- 1 white onion, sliced
- 2 Vidalia onions, sliced
- 4-6 fresh garlic cloves, diced
- 2 tbsp pickling salt
- 1 tbsp mustard seed
- 1 tbsp celery seed
- 1 tbsp pickling spice
- 4-7 chili peppers, fresh
- 3 cups white vinegar
- 1 cup cider vinegar
- 1 cup water
- 24 hard-boiled eggs, peeled (48 pullet eggs)

Preparation Method

1. Put onions and garlic in a saucepan.
2. Add the remaining ingredients except eggs and bring them to boil.
3. Place peeled eggs, onions, garlic, and uncut peppers into hot jars, glass, then pour in hot sauce.
4. Place lids immediately. Wipe the jar rims with clean damp cloth.
5. Process in boiling water in a pressure canner for about 15 minutes.
6. Cool to seal.

Calories 174, Total fat 10.8g, Saturated 3.3g, Total carbs 3.6g, Net carbs 3.1g, Protein 13.7g, Sugars 1.8g, Fiber 0.5g, Sodium 728mg, Potassium 216mg

Pickled Jalapenos

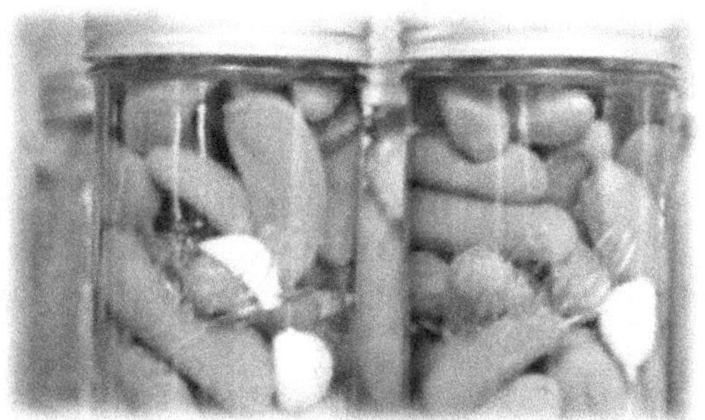

This is another perfect recipe for beginners. Pickled jalapenos are an easy recipe to make and it makes only 2 jars of spicy and delicious pickled jalapenos rings. Try it.

Prep time: 50 minutes, **Cook time:** 10 minutes, **Process time:** 10 minutes; **Serves** 2

Ingredients

- 3-1/2 cups white vinegar
- 1 cup of water
- 1 tbsp pickling salt
- 1-1/2 lbs jalapenos peppers, washed and stems cut off

Preparation Method

1. Combine the vinegar, water, and salt in a saucepan, medium. Bring to a boil for about 5 minutes.
2. Place pepper into hot jars then ladle hot brine into the jars. Leave 1/2 -inch headspace.
3. Remove air bubbles using non-metal utensils and add more brine but maintain headspace.
4. Wipe the jar rims using a clean damp cloth.
5. Place the jars in a pressure canner and process for about 10 minutes following manufacturers' guide and depending on the altitude.

Nutritional Information

Calories 765, Total fat 7.7g, Saturated fat 0.8g, Total carbs 90.9g, Net carbs 56g, Protein 16.8g, Sugars 50.6g, Fiber 34.9g, Sodium 2989mg, Potassium 4041mg

Canned Spicy Garlic Pickled Carrots

These canned pickled carrots are great as a snack all winter long. It is a delicious recipe as carrots are great vegetables to match with brine. Enjoy this great appetizer.

Prep time: 15 minutes, **Cook time:** 25 minutes, **Process time:** 15 minutes; **Serves** 4

Ingredients

- 8-1/2 cups fresh garden carrots, small and peeled
- 5-1/2 cups white vinegar, distilled
- 2 cups of sugar
- 3 Garlic cloves
- 1 cup water
- 2 tbsp canning salt
- 3 tbsp pickling spice

Preparation Method

1. Wash and peel carrots well.
2. In the meantime, combine vinegar, sugar, garlic, water, and salt in a stockpot, large, bring to a gentle boil for about 3 minutes.
3. Add carrots and boil again. Reduce heat and simmer for about 10 minutes until carrots are half-cooked.
4. Divide spice among 4 jars then fill the hot jars with hot carrots and leave 1-inch headspace.
5. Scoop pickling liquid into the jars covering the carrots. Leave 1/2-inch headspace.
6. Poke a knife through liquid and carrots to remove air bubbles adjusting headspace if necessary.
7. Wipe jar rims with a clean damp paper towel then apply 2-pieces canning lids.
8. Process the jars in a pressure canner for about 15 minutes following the manufacturer's guide and according to altitude.

Nutritional Information

Calories 557, Total fat 0g, Saturated fat 0g, Total carbs 125g, Net carbs 117g, Protein 2g, Sugars 112g, Fiber 8g, Sodium 1389mg, Potassium 691mg

Canned Spicy Pickled Asparagus

This is an easy recipe to make and can asparagus pickles that you can

have in your salads, cheese plates, and appetizers. You will fall in love with canned asparagus.
Prep time: 40 minutes, **Cook time:** 10 minutes, **Process time:** 10 minutes; **Serves** 7

Ingredients

- 5 cups water
- 5 tbsp pickling salt
- 5 tbsp sugar
- 5 cups vinegar
- 7 halved garlic cloves, large
- 10-12 lbs asparagus

Preparation Method

1. Add and stir well water, salt, sugar, and vinegar in a pot, non-reactive. Boil slowly.
2. Place garlic cloves to the jars bottom then fill with asparagus spears .They should be packed tight.
3. Fill the hot jars with hot vinegar mixture. Leave 1/2 -inch headspace.
4. Remove any air bubbles using a wooden spatula then add more vinegar mixture if needed but maintain the headspace. Now wipe the jar rims using a clean damp towel.
5. Place lids and rings and tighten to fingertip tight.
6. Place the jars in a pressure

canner and process for about 10 minutes following manufacturers' guide and according to the altitude.

Nutritional Information

Calories 49, Total fat 0.2g, Saturated fat 0.1g, Total carbs 8.7g, Net carbs 5.3g, Protein 3.6g, Sugars 4.9g, Fiber 3.4g, Sodium 318mg, Potassium 262mg

Sweet and Spicy Pickled Radishes

This is a simple and perfect canning recipe that involves pickling and canning all varieties of radishes.
Prep time: 30 minutes, **Cook time:** 10 minutes, **Process time:** 10 minutes; **Serves** 6

Ingredients

- 1-1/2 cups water
- 2 tbsp canning salt
- 1-1/4 cups white vinegar
- 3/4 cup raw sugar

- 1/4 cup red wine vinegar
- 2 tbsp mixed peppercorns
- 1 tbsp mustard seeds
- 1 tbsp red pepper flakes, dried
- 2 lbs radishes, 1/8 -inch thick

Preparation Method

1. Combine all ingredients except radishes in a saucepan, medium. Bring to a boil over high-medium heat until salt and sugar dissolves.
2. Place radishes into hot pint jars and leave 1/2 -inch headspace.
3. Scoop hot vinegar mixture into the jars and leave 1/2 -inch headspace then distribute seeds, peppercorns, and flakes among the jars.
4. Wipe the jar rims with a clean damp cloth. Place lids and rings and tighten to fingertip tight.
5. Process jars in a pressure canner and process for about 10 minutes following manufacturers guide and according to the altitude.

Nutritional Information

Calories 142, Total fat 0.9g, Saturated fat 0.1g, Total carbs 33.2g, Net carbs 29.7g, Protein 1.8g, Sugars 28.3g, Fiber 3.5g, Sodium 1990mg, Potassium 456mg

Pickled Cherry Tomatoes

This is one of the simplest canning recipes to make. Pickled cherry tomatoes is a combination of garden veggies and tomatoes for quite long term storage.

Prep time: 30 minutes, **Cook time:** 15 minutes, **Process time:** 15 minutes; **Serves** 7

Ingredients

- 4-1/2 cups water
- 4 cups vinegar
- 1 cup sugar
- 6 tbsp canning salt
- 8 cups cherry tomatoes
- 2 cups coarsely chopped celery
- 4 cups coarsely chopped onion
- 2 cups coarsely chopped sweet pepper
- **Optional:** 1 cup cucamelon
- 6-7 garlic cloves
- 6-7 heads of dill

1. Combine water, vinegar, salt, and sugar in a saucepot, large, then boil.
2. Pack the vegetables to your hot jars and leave 1/4 -inch headspace. To each jar, add 1 garlic clove and 1 head of dill.
3. Scoop hot liquid into the hot jars and leave 1/4 -inch headspace.
4. Now remove air bubbles checking headspace.
5. Wipe jar rims with a clean damp cloth and apply 2-piece caps.
6. Process in a pressure canner for about 15 minutes following the manufacturer's guide and according to the altitude.

Nutritional Information

Calories 72, Total fat 0.2g, Saturated fat 0.1g, Total carbs 15.5g, Net carbs 10.5g, Protein 0.8g, Sugars 13.4g, Fiber 5g, Sodium 2256mg, Potassium 1789m

Canned Garlic Dill Pickles

Are you a beginner? Canning dill pickles are a great and one of the easiest starters for you. It is a recipe that you will enjoy making and canning.

Prep time: 45 minutes, **Cook time:** 15 minutes, **Process time:** 10 minutes; **Serves** 15

Ingredients

- 3 lbs onions
- 20 lbs sliced pickling cucumbers, whole or speared
- 22 cups water
- 10 cups white vinegar
- 1-1/3 cup pickling salt
- 45 garlic cloves, peeled
- 1 sprigs fresh dill
- 45 peppercorns

Preparation Method

1. Layer onions and cucumber in a bowl, large, then cover with salt. Top them with ice cubes then

cover and refrigerate for about 2 hours.

2. Drain well and rinse well. Use a colander to rinse and drain.
3. Combine water, vinegar, and pickling salt then boil.
4. Add 3 garlic cloves and 1 fresh dill sprig to each hot quart jar then fill with onions and cucumbers.
5. Ladle hot vinegar mixture to the hot jar and leave 1/2-inch headspace.
6. Release any air bubbles then wipe jar rims. Place lids and rings on.
7. Place the jars in a pressure canner and process for about 10 minutes following manufacturers guide and according to altitude.

Nutritional Information

Calories 175, Total fat 0.8g, Saturated fat 0.2g, Total carbs 35.2g, Net carbs 29.9g, Protein 5.6g, Sugars 14.7g, Fiber 5.3g, Sodium 2564mg, Potassium 1189mg

Pickled Cauliflower

This is a healthy canning recipe that you have to come across. Pickled cauliflower is easy to make and can in a pressure canner that your family will be left yearning for more. Enjoy it.

Prep time: 30 minutes, **Cook time:** 10 minutes, **Process time:** 10 minutes; **Serves** 12

Ingredients

- 2-1/2 lbs cauliflower florets
- quart white wine vinegar
- 2 thinly sliced onions, medium
- 1/2 tbsp red pepper flakes, hot
- 2 cups sugar

Preparation Method

1. Boil a pot of water over high heat then add 1/4 cup pickling salt.
2. Add the florets and bring to a boil for 3 minutes then drain.
3. Combine vinegar, onions, pepper flakes, and sugar in a medium pot, nonreactive while swirling

until sugar is dissolved.

4. Boil over low-medium heat gently for about 5 minutes then remove from heat.
5. Pack florets and onions into hot jars then cover with the vinegar solution.Make sure pepper flakes are evenly distributed. Leave 1/2 -inch headspace.
6. Wipe the rims of the jars then set lids and rings ensuring fingertip tightness.
7. Place the jars in a pressure canner and process for about 10 minutes following manufacturers guide and according to altitude.

Nutritional information

Calories 249, Total fat 0.5g, Saturated fat 0.1g, Total carbs 56.9g, Net carbs 46.5g, Protein 8.1g, Sugars 44g, Fiber 10.4g, Sodium 124mg, Potassium 1292mg

Pickled Red Grapes

These pickled grapes are great and goes well with cheese, topped on baked ricotta, makes an addition to roasted meat dishes and as an addition to salads.

Prep time: 30 minutes, **Cook time:** 10 minutes, **Process time:** 15 minutes; **Serves** 3

Ingredients

- 2 cups red wine vinegar
- 2 cups water
- 2 cups sugar
- 6 allspice berries
- 12 black peppercorns
- 3 ginger slices
- 2 lb red grapes

Preparation Method

1. Combine vinegar, water and sugar in a small saucepan, non reactive, over low heat while stirring until sugar dissolves. Increase heat and bring to a boil then remove from heat.
2. Put berries, 4 peppercorns and 1 ginger slice into each hot jar.
3. Now pack the grapes carefully and tightly into the jars.
4. Add vinegar solution to each jar leaving 1/2 -inch headspace then remove air bubbles if any.
5. Wipe the jar rims using a clean damp cloth and place lids and rings making its fingertip tight.
6. Process the jars in a pressure canner for about 15 minutes

following the manufacturer's
guide and according to altitude.

Nutritional Information

Calories 781, Total fat 1.2g,
Saturated fat 0.3g, Total carbs
199.1g, Net carbs 194.2g, Protein
2.9g, Sugars 180.1g, Fiber 4.9g,
Sodium 24mg, Potassium 848mg

CHAPTER 9: James, Jellies and preserve

Canned Apple Preserves

This is a gorgeous and delicious apple preserve that can be served on so many types of meat or on toast.

Prep time: 10 minutes, **Cook time:** 5 minutes, **Process time:** 5 minutes: **Serves** 6 pints

Ingredients

- 6 cups apples, peeled, cored and sliced
- 1 tbsp lemon juice
- 1 cup water
- 1 pack powdered pectin
- 1/2 lemon, thinly sliced
- 4 cups sugar
- 2 tbsp nutmeg

Preparation Method

1. Add apples, lemon juice, and water in a saucepan. Simmer covered for 10 minutes.
2. Stir in powdered pectin and bring to boil. Let boil for 1minute while stirring frequently.
3. Add lemon and sugar in the saucepan and let boil for 1 more minute while stirring frequently.
4. Remove the mixture from heat and add nutmeg.
5. Add the hot preserve in sterilized pint jars leaving a 1/4 inch headspace.
6. Wipe rims with a damp paper towel. Adjust the jar lids then place the jars in the pressure canner with water such that the jars are covered by water at least 2-inch.
7. Cover the pressure canner with an ordinary lid that fits snugly and process the jars for 5 minutes.
8. Wait for the canner to cool before removing the jars.

Nutritional Information

Calories 31, Total fat 0.1g, Saturated fat 0g, Total carbs 7.3g, Net carbs 4.3g Protein 0.1, Sugars 0g, Fiber

0.6g, Sodium 5.3mg, Potassium 19.9mg

Canned Apricot Jam

If you have a big family and love saving money then this is one great recipe you should try. Pack your pantry with this fun to make and delicious apricot jam for toasts.
Prep time: 10 minutes, **Cook time:** 5 minutes, **Process time:** 5 minutes: **Serves** 5 pints

Ingredients

- 2 quarts apricots crushed, crushed
- 1/4 cup lemon juice
- 6 cups sugar

Preparation Method

1. Combine all the ingredients in a pot and bring to boil while stirring occasionally until all sugar has dissolved.
2. Cook rapidly on high heat for 25 minutes or until the mixture thickens. Stir frequently to prevent it from sticking.
3. Remove from heat and fill the sterilized pint jars with the hot jam leaving a 1/4 inch headspace.
4. Wipe the rims with damp cloth and place the lids on the jars.
5. Place the jars in the pressure canner with water such that the jars are covered by water at least 2-inch.
6. Cover the pressure canner with an ordinary lid that fits snugly and process the jars for 5 minutes .Wait for the canner to cool before removing the jars.

Nutritional Information

Calories 48, Total fat 0.1g, Saturated fat 0g, Total carbs 12.9g, Net carbs 12.8g Protein 0.1, Sugars 0g, Fiber 0.1g, Sodium 8mg, Potassium 15mg

Canned Fig Jam

This easy to preserve fig jam is all you need on toast for breakfast. It's so yummy that you will want more and more if not forgetting that it's packed with nutrients.

Prep time: 20 minutes, **Cook time:** 10 minutes, **Process time:** 5 minutes: **Serves** 5 pints

Ingredients

- 2 quarts figs, freshly chopped
- 6 cups sugar
- 3/4 cup water
- 1/4 cup lemon juice

Preparation Method

1. Place figs in a stockpot and add boiling water over them. Let rest for 10 minutes, then drain the water, stem, and chop the figs.
2. Add sugar and water to the figs. Bring to boil while stirring occasionally until all sugar dissolves.
3. Cook rapidly while stirring frequently until the mixture thickens. Add lemon juice and cook for 1 more minute.
4. Pour the hot fig jam in sterilized pint jars leaving a 1/4 inch headspace. Wipe the rims with a damp cloth and place the lids on the jars.
5. Place the jars in the pressure canner with water such that the jars are covered by water at least 2-inches.
6. Cover the pressure canner with an ordinary lid that fits snugly and process the jars for 5 minutes.
7. Wait for the canner to cool before removing the jars. Let the jars rest on a cooling rack before storing in a cool dry place.

Nutritional Information

Calories 61, Total fat 0.1g, Saturated fat 0g, Total carbs 0g, Net carbs 0g Protein 0.1, Sugars 0g, Fiber 0g, Sodium 30mg, Potassium 100mg

Canned Tutti- frutti Jam

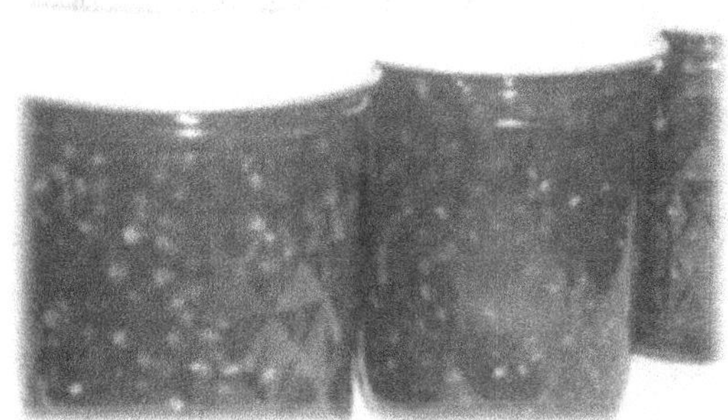

This fabulous frutti tutti jam is a great way to add sugars or calories in your body. Your family and friends will be delighted when you serve

them this jam over Italian toast for breakfast.

Prep time: 20 minutes, **Cook time:** 10 minutes, **Process time:** 5 minutes: **Serves** 3 pints

Ingredients

- 3 cups pears, chopped
- 1 orange
- 1/4 cups maraschino cherries, chopped
- 3/4 cup crushed pineapple, drained
- 1/4 cup lemon juice
- 1 pack powdered pectin
- 5 cups sugar

Preparation Method

1. Sort the pears then wash them thoroughly. Pare, core then chop the pears.
2. Peel the oranges, deseed then grind pulp or chop them.
3. Add the pears into a kettle then add the oranges, cherries, pineapples and lemon juice.
4. Add in pectin and give a good stir. Place the kettle over high heat and heat while stirring constantly until the mixture comes to a full boil.
5. Add sugar and continue heating while stirring until boiling. Let boil for 1 minute then remove from heat and skim.
6. Fill the sterilized jars with the jam leaving a 1/4 headspace. Wipe the rims with damp clean cloth and place the lids on the jars.
7. Place the jars in the pressure canner with water such that the jars are covered by water at least 2-inches.
8. Cover the pressure canner with an ordinary lid that fits well and process the jars for 5 minutes .Wait for the canner to cool before removing the jars.

Nutritional Information

Calories 127, Total fat 0g, Saturated fat 0g, Total carbs 0g, Net carbs 0g Protein 0.1g, Sugars 29g, Fiber 0g, Sodium 0mg, Potassium 0mg

Grape-Plum Jelly

If you are a jelly lover or simply a plum lover, then you have to try this

grape plum jelly that is easy but very tasteful.

Prep time: 20 minutes, **Cook time:** 10 minutes, **Process time:** 5 minutes: **Serves** 5 pints

Ingredients

- 3-1/2 lb plums, ripe
- 3 lb concord grapes, ripe
- 1 cup water
- 1/2 tbsp butter
- 1-3/4 oz powdered pectin
- 8-1/2 cups sugar

Preparation Method

1. Wash the plums with clean water.
2. Crush the plums and the grapes thoroughly in a pan with water, do it one layer at a time.
3. Bring the mixture to a boil then reduce heat and simmer for 10 minutes. Add the mixture to a jelly bath and strain the liquid.
4. Add 6-1/2 cup of the liquid, butter and pectin in a pan. Bring to boil while stirring over high heat.
5. Add sugar and return to boiling while stirring until all sugar has dissolved. Remove from heat and skim any foam.
6. Fill the sterilized jars with the hot grape plum jelly, leaving a 1/4 headspace. Wipe the rims with damp clean cloth and close the lids
7. Place the jars in the pressure canner with water such that the jars are covered by water at least 2-inches.
8. Cover the pressure canner with an ordinary lid that fits well and process the jars for 5 minutes.
9. Wait for the canner to cool before removing the jars.

Nutritional Information

Calories 46, Total fat 0g, Saturated fat 0g, Total carbs 9g, Net carbs 7g Protein 0g, Sugars 0g, Fiber 2g, Sodium 0mg, Potassium 0mg

Plum Jelly

Prep time: 20 minutes, **Cook time:** 10 minutes, **Process time:** 5 minutes: **Serves** 4 pints

Ingredients

- 5 cups plum juice
- 1pack powdered pectin

- 7 cups sugar

Preparation Method

1. Sort and thoroughly wash the plums with clean water. Cut the plums into pieces.
2. Crush the plums and add water and bring to boil while covered. Reduce heat and simmer for 10 minutes. Strain the juice.
3. Add the juice in a kettle and add powdered pectin and stir well. Cook over high heat while stirring constantly until it boils.
4. Add sugar and continue to cook while stirring until boiling and all sugar has dissolved.
5. Pour the hot jelly in the sterilized jars leaving a 1/4 headspace. Wipe the rims with damp clean cloth and close the lids
6. Place the jars in the pressure canner with water such that the jars are covered by water at least 2-inches.
7. Cover the pressure canner with an ordinary lid that fits well and process the jars for 5 minutes. Wait for the canner to cool before removing the jars.

Nutritional Information

Calories 37, Total fat 0g, Saturated fat 0g, Total carbs 9.5g, Net carbs 9.5g Protein 0.1g, Sugars 8.3g, Fiber 0g, Sodium 0mg, Potassium 0.2mg

Canned Strawberry Jelly

Do you know that strawberries are sweetest in the spring which is definitely the best time to make this strawberry jelly. Most importantly, its perfect when cutting on weight **Prep time:** 20 minutes, **Cook time:** 10 minutes, **Process time:** 5 minutes: **Serves** 4 pints

Ingredients

- 4 cups strawberry juice
- 7-1/2 cup sugar
- 2 pouches liquid pectin

Preparation Method

1. Wash the strawberries thoroughly removing any stem or caps. crush them and extract juice.
2. Add the strawberry juice and sugar into a kettle. Give a good

stir and heat until the mixture
cannot be stirred down.

3. Add pectin and continue heating
   until it boils. Boil hard for a
   minute then skim off any foam.
4. Pour the strawberry jelly in the
   sterilized jars leaving a 1/4
   headspace. Wipe the rims with
   damp cloth and close the lids
5. Place the jars in the pressure
   canner with water such that the
   jars are covered by water at
   least 2-inches.
6. Cover the pressure canner with
   an ordinary lid that fits well and
   process the jars for 5 minutes.

Nutritional Information

Calories 46, Total fat 0g, Saturated
fat 0g, Total carbs 10g, Net carbs 9g
Protein 0g, Sugars 0g, Fiber 1g,
Sodium 0mg, Potassium 0mg

Batia Palm Fruit Jelly

Whether you want to make this jelly
in small or in large batches, it is
perfect for you. A few minutes and
your pantry is packed with this batia
palm fruit jelly.

Prep time: 40 minutes, **Cook time:**
50 minutes, **Process time:** 10
minutes: **Serves** 4 pints

Ingredients

- 3 quarts ripe fruit
- 6 cups water
- 1 pack powdered pectin
- Food colour drops
- 7-1/2 cups sugar

Preparation Method

1. Sort the fruits and wash them
   while removing sepals and
   stems if any. Add them in a pot
   with water and bring them to boil
   while covered. Reduce heat and
   simmer for 30 minutes.
2. Crush The fruit using a potato
   masher even though the seeds
   are too large so the masher
   partially crashes.
3. Collect the juice that drains
   through the colander then strain
   the juice. Refrigerate the juice
   overnight.
4. Pour off the juice leaving the
   residue. Measure 5-1/2 cups of
   the strained juice and pour it
   into a shallow saucepan.

5. Stir in powdered until well dissolved. Add pectin and bring to a boil while stirring occasionally.
6. Add sugar and heat as you stir until it has all dissolved. Bring the mixture to a hard boiling while stirring constantly.
7. Remove from heat and transfer the jelly to sterilized jars leaving a 1/4 inch headspace.
8. Wipe the rims with damp cloth and close the lids
9. Place the jars in the pressure canner with water such that the jars are covered by water at least 2-inches.
10. Cover the pressure canner with an ordinary lid that fits well and process the jars for 10 minutes .

Nutritional Information

Calories 127, Total fat 0g, Saturated fat 0g, Total carbs 0g, Net carbs 0g Protein 0.1g, Sugars 29g, Fiber 0g, Sodium 0mg, Potassium 0mg

Pear preserves

This pear preserve is so good that everyone will love more and more of it. I hope you enjoy it as much as I do.

Prep time: 40 minutes, **Cook time:** 40 minutes, **Process time:** 5 minutes: **Serves** 3 pints

Ingredients

- 3 cups cups sugar
- 2-1/2 cups water
- 6 ripe pears, cored and cut in quarters
- 1 lemon, thinly sliced

Preparation Method

1. Mix half of the sugar and water in a pot and cook over high heat for 2 minutes.
2. Add pears and boil for 15 minutes. Add the remaining sugar and lemon to the sugar mixture. Mix until all sugar has dissolved. Cook for 25 more minutes .

3. Cover and refrigerate for 12-24 minutes.
4. Heat the mixture until boiling then remove from heat. Pack it in the sterilized jars.
5. Wipe the jar rims with a damp cloth and close the lids
6. Place the jars in the pressure canner with water such that the jars are covered by water at least 2-inches.
7. Cover the pressure canner with an ordinary lid that fits well and process the jars for 5 minutes.
8. Let the canner rest to cool before removing the jars and cooling them on a rack. Store your preserve in a cool dry place.

Nutritional Information

Calories 50, Total fat 0g, Saturated fat 0g, Total carbs 12g, Net carbs 12g Protein 0g, Sugars 10g, Fiber 0g, Sodium 0mg, Potassium 0mg

Watermelon Rind Preserves

This is a delicious preserve that is easy to make and that you will love. The secret is to have watermelons with a thick ring

Prep time: 30 minutes, **Cook time:** 70 minutes, **Process time:** 5 minutes: **Serves** 3 pints

Ingredients

- 1-1/2 watermelon rinds pieces, trimmed
- 4 tbsp salt
- 2 quarts cold water
- 1 tbsp ginger. Ground
- 4 cups sugar
- 1/4 cup lemon juice
- 7 cups water
- 1 lemon, thinly sliced

Preparation Method

1. Trim the pink flesh and the green skin from the watermelon rind. Cut the rind into 1-inch pieces.
2. Mix salt and water in a mixing bowl then pour the mixture over the watermelon rinds.

Refrigerate for 6 hours.

3. Drain the watermelon rinds, rinse and drain them again with clean water. Add water to the rinds and let them sit for 30 minutes.
4. Drain the water and sprinkle ground ginger. Add more water until covered then cook until tender. Drain the water.
5. Add sugar, lemon juice, and water in a saucepan and bring to boil for 5 minutes.
6. Add the rinds and boil for 30 more minutes. Add the sliced lemon and cook until the lemon slices are clear.
7. Add the hot mixture in sterilized jars then wipe the jar rims with a clean cloth.
8. Place the jars in the pressure canner with water such that the jars are covered by water at least 2-inches.
9. Cover the pressure canner with an ordinary lid that fits well and process the jars for 5 minutes.
10. Let the canner rest to cool before removing the jars. Store your watermelon rind preserve in a cool dry place.

Nutritional Information

Calories 25, Total fat 0g, Saturated fat 0g, Total carbs 7g, Net carbs 0g Protein 0.1g, Sugars 5g, Fiber 0g, Sodium 0mg, Potassium 0mg

CHAPTER 10: Salads and Relishes

Canned Zucchini Salad

This is a delicious old Russian zucchini recipe that uses zucchini, peppers and tomatoes spiced up with a lot of garlic to make a delish salad.

Prep time: 30 minutes, **Cook time:** 30 minutes, **Process time:** 20 minutes: **Serves** 6 pints

Ingredients

- 6 cups zucchini, diced
- 7-1/2 cups tomato
- 4 big bell peppers
- 1/2 cup sugar
- 1 tbsp oil
- 5 garlic cloves
- 1 tbsp salt
- 1 cup vinegar

Preparation Method

1. Dice zucchini into half inch cubes then slice the tomatoes and peppers.
2. Cook tomatoes with sugar for 10 minutes then add zucchini, peppers and oil.
3. Cook for 10 more minutes. Add garlic, salt and vinegar then cook for 10 more minutes.
4. Ladle into sterilized pint jars, wipe the jar rims and close the lids.
5. Process in boiling water in the pressure canner for 20 minutes.

Nutritional Information

Calories 76, Total fat 3.8g, Saturated fat 0.5g, Total carbs 10.5g, Net carbs 7.4g Protein 1.8g, Sugars 3g, Fiber 3.1g, Sodium 11mg, Potassium 541mg

Canned Three Bean Salad

This yummy three bean salad is a great treat side dish that uses yellow wax beans, green bush beans and dry beans.its the best salad to serve your family and is very satisfying

Prep time: 10 minutes, **Cook time:** 15 minutes, **Process time:** 5 minutes: **Serves** 3 pints

- 1-1/2 lb green bush beans
- 1-1/2 lb yellow wax beans
- 3 cups cooked red kidney beans
- 1 red garden onion, sliced
- 6 peppers banana
- Boiling water
- 2-1/2 cup granulated sugar
- 1 tbsp mustard seeds
- 1 tbsp celery seeds
- 4 tbsp pickling salt
- 3 cups white vinegar
- 1-1/4 cup distilled water

1. Add all the beans, onions and peppers in a saucepan. Add water until covered then bring to boil over medium heat. Reduce heat to simmer for 5 minutes or until the veggies are heated through.
2. In a separate saucepan, combine sugar, mustard seed, celery seeds, salt, white vinegar, and distilled water. Bring to boil until the sugar has dissolved. Reduce heat and simmer until all spices have been fully infused.
3. Drain the vegetables and pack them in the sterilized pint jars leaving a 1/2 inch headspace. Remove the air bubble and add the cooking liquid if necessary.
4. Wipe the rims and place the lids.
5. Process the jars in boiling water in the pressure canner for 15 minutes.
6. Remove the jars from the canner and let rest to cool before storing in a cool dry place.

Calories 185, Total fat 7.8g, Saturated fat 0.7g, Total carbs 27g, Net carbs 23.3g Protein 3.4g,

Sugars 18g, Fiber 3.7g, Sodium 242mg, Potassium 254mg

Prize Winning Canned Zucchini Relish

Has zucchini taken over in your garden? If yes then this fantastic, sweet zucchini relish is the recipe for you.

Prep time: 30 minutes, **Cook time:** 20 minutes, **Process time:** 5 minutes: **Serves** 5 pints

- 10 cups zucchini, chopped
- 4 cups onions, chopped
- 1 red pepper, chopped
- 4 oz green chile, chopped
- 3 tbsp canning salt
- 3-1/2 cup sugar
- 3 cups vinegar
- 1 tbsp turmeric , ground
- 4 celery seeds
- 1 tbsp pepper
- 1/2 tbsp nutmeg, ground

Preparation Method

1. Combine zucchini, chopped onions, red pepper, chilies and canning salt in a mixing bowl. Stir well until combined then chill overnight. Rinse well and drain.
2. Combine all other ingredients in a large kettle and bring to boil. Add zucchini mixture, reduce heat and simmer for 10 minutes.
3. Scoop the hot mixture into sterilized jars leaving a 1/4 inch headspace. Wipe the rims and adjust the lids.
4. Process the jars in boiling water in the pressure canner for 15 minutes.
5. Remove the jars from the canner and let rest to cool before storing in a cool dry place.

Nutritional Information

Calories 693.6, Total fat 1.7g, Saturated fat 0.4g, Total carbs 165.8g, Net carbs 159.5g Protein 5.7g, Sugars 154.1g, Fiber 6.3g, Sodium 4221.2mg

Beetroot Relish

This is an easy recipe for homegrown produce. Serve these beets relish with cold meats, cheese and sandwiches.

Prep time: 30 minutes, **Cook time:** 50 minutes, **Process time:** 10 minutes: **Serves** 3 pints

Ingredients

- 700g beetroot
- 1 red onion, finely chopped
- 1 cup CSR jams sugar
- 1-1/2 cups white vinegar
- Pinch salt
- 1/2 tbsp black pepper

Preparation Method

1. Put a pot of water over heat and bring it to boil.
2. Clean the beets and cut off the leaves or stems. Place the beets in the boiling water for 20 minutes.
3. Remove the beets from the hot water and let cool. Wear gloves and remove the skin from beets ten grate them into a mixing bowl.
4. Add the grated beets and all other ingredients in a pot and heat over low heat until the sugar dissolves.
5. Let the mixture simmer for 30 minutes or until some liquid has evaporated and the mixture has a jam consistency.
6. Pour the relish in sterilized jars and process the jars in boiling water in the pressure canner for 10 minutes.
7. Remove the jars from the canner and let rest to cool before storing in a cool dry place.

Nutritional Information

Calories 0, Total fat 0g, Saturated fat 0g, Total carbs 0g, Net carbs 0g Protein 0g, Sugars 0g, Fiber 0g, Sodium 0mg, Potassium 0mg

Spicy Tomato relish

This tomato recipe is tangy, spicy and packed with flavors that explode in your mouth. You can also make this relish for a gift basket during holidays

Prep time: 5 minutes, **Cook time:** 20 minutes, **Process time:** 5 minutes: **Serves** 3 pints

Ingredients

- 6 tomatoes
- 10g Indian chili powder plus 1 tbsp
- 1 tbsp sugar
- 1 tbsp salt
- 4 tbsp sesame seed oil

Preparation Method

1. Dice the tomatoes and them in a Dutch oven.
2. Add all other ingredients and cook over medium heat for 30 minutes or until the mixture thickens.
3. The oil should be separating from the mixture on the side. Scoop the oil with a spoon and put in the sterized pint jar.
4. Process the jars in hot water for 10 minutes then cool completely.
5. Store in a cool dry place.

Nutritional Information

Calories 40, Total fat 3.5g, Saturated fat 0g, Total carbs 2g, Net carbs 1g Protein 0g, Sugars 2g, Fiber 0.5g, Sodium 150mg, Potassium 100mg

Dill Pickle Relish

This is the best relish to serve your family come summer time. Dill pickle relish fans shovel it on hot dogs which is insanely addictive

Prep time: 15 minutes, **Cook time:** 10 minutes, **Process time:** 15 minutes: **Serves** 4 pints

Ingredients

- 8 lb pickling cucumbers

- 6 oz pickling salt
- 2-1/2 cup onion
- 1 litre white vinegar
- 16 oz sugar
- 1 tbsp celery seeds
- 1 tbsp mustard seed
- 3 drops green coloring

1. Wash the cucumbers thoroughly under running water then trim off the ends. Chop into large pieces the pulse in a food processor until finely chopped.
2. Transfer the cucumber into a large pot and sprinkle with salt. Mix the vegetables and more salt using your hands.
3. Top with water such that everything is covered and let stand for 2 hours.
4. Meanwhile prepare the onions and set aside.
5. Drain the cucumbers and rinse with clean water. Mix everything in a large pot and bring to boil for 10 minutes.
6. Pack the mixture in sterilized hot jars leaving a 1/2 inch headspace.
7. Process the jars in boiling water in a pressure canner for 15 minutes.

Nutritional Information

Calories 23, Total fat 0.1g, Saturated fat 0g, Total carbs 5.6g, Net carbs 5.3g Protein 0.3g, Sugars 4.7g, Fiber 0.3g, Sodium 63mg, Potassium 0mg

Sweet and Spicy Pickle relish

This is a versatile, tasty pickle relish that you can use on your sandwich or stir into chicken or tuna salad.
Prep time: 35 minutes, **Cook time:** 35 minutes, **Process time:** 10 minutes: **Serves** 2 pints

Ingredients

- 3 cups green pepper, grated
- 3 cups pickling cucumber
- 1cup onions, minced
- 2 cups cider vinegar
- 1 cup granulated sugar
- 1 tbsp salt
- 1 tbsp mustard seed
- 1/2 tbsp celery seed
- 1 tbsp red chili flakes

Preparation Method

1. Mix peppers, cucumber, and onions in a pot. Add a cup of cider vinegar and bring simmer for 30 minutes while stirring occasionally until the vegetables have reduced by a third.
2. Add the remaining vinegar, granulated sugar, and spies. Simmer for 5 more minutes and remove from heat.
3. Pack the relish in sterilized jars and process in boiling water in the pressure canner for 10 minutes.
4. Let cool on a countertop lined with a towel before storing the in a cool dry place.

Nutritional Information

Calories 36.1, Total fat 0g, Saturated fat 0g, Total carbs 10g, Net carbs 10g Protein 0g, Sugars 9g, Fiber 0g, Sodium 227.1mg, Potassium 0mg

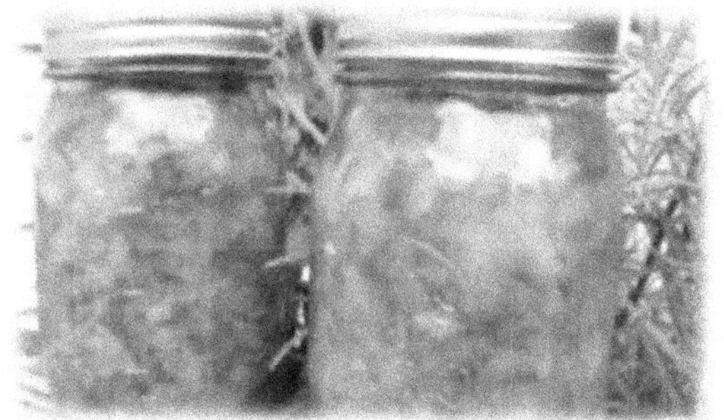

Canned Pepper Relish

This is an eye- catching medley that boost the flavours instantly.its perfect on potato salads, coleslaw, and barbecued sandwich. It's also great when heated on pork or chiken breast

Prep time: 20minutes, **Cook time:** 10 minutes, **Process time:** 10 minutes: **Serves** 1 pint

Ingredients

- 2 tbsp green chilies, chopped
- 1/4 cup each green, red and yellow pepper, finely chopped
- 1 tbsp jalapeno pepper
- 3 tbsp chopped onions, finely chopped
- 1/2 cup water
- 1/2 tbsp salt
- 1 small bay leaf
- 1/8 tbsp coriander
- 1/4 tbsp allspice, ground
- 3 tbsp white vinegar
- 2 tbsp sugar

Preparation Method

1. Place the chilies, peppers and onions in a glass container.
2. Bring Water and salt to boil in a saucepan then pour the salted hot water over the pepper mixture.
3. Stir in the bay leaf. Coriander and allspice and refrigerate overnight.

4. Bring vinegar and sugar to boil then reduce heat and simmer for 4 minutes or until all sugar has dissolved.
5. Drain the pepper mixture discarding the bay leaves and transfer the mixture in sterilized hot pint jars. Pour over the vinegar mixture.
6. Process the jars in hot water in the pressure canner for 10 minutes.
7. Let the jars cool before labeling and storing them.

Nutritional Information

Calories 36, Total fat 0g, Saturated fat 0g, Total carbs 9g, Net carbs 8g Protein 0g, Sugars 7g, Fiber 1g, Sodium 0mg, Potassium 0mg

Green Tomato Relish

Prep time: 5 minutes, **Cook time:** 20 minutes, **Process time:** 5 minutes: **Serves** 4 pints

Ingredients

- 5 kg green tomatoes
- 6 cups onions
- 1.25 kg bell peppers, finely chopped
- 1/2 cup pickling salt
- 1 litre water
- 1 litre vinegar
- 2 tbsp cornstarch
- 4 cups sugar
- 1/3 cup mustard

Preparation Method

1. Add tomatoes, onions, and pepper in a pot then add water and salt. Bring to boil, and then simmer for 5 minutes.
2. Drain the water and transfer the veggies to a saucepan.
3. Whisk portion vinegar into cornstarch. Add the cornstarch mixture into the veggies. Let the mixture rest for some minutes.
4. Bring to boil and then simmer for 5 minutes. Pack the mixture in sterilized pint jars leaving a headspace of 1/2 inch.
5. Wipe the jar rims with a damp cloth then put on the lids.
6. Process the jars in a canner for 5 minutes at 10 pounds pressure.

Calories 41, Total fat 0.2g, Saturated fat 0g, Total carbs 9.9g, Net carbs 9.1g Protein 0.5g, Sugars 8.8g, Fiber 0.8g, Sodium 544mg

Vidalia Onion Relish

Prep time: 5 minutes, **Cook time:** 20 minutes, **Process time:** 5 minutes: **Serves** 3 pints

Ingredients

- 5 lb sweet onions, slices
- 2 tbsp sea salt
- 2 cups apple cider vinegar
- 1 cup granulated sugar
- 1 tbsp mustard seeds
- 1 tbsp red chili flakes
- 1/2 tbsp turmeric

Preparation Method

1. Put the onions in a large mixing bowl and add salt. Use hands to massage the salt on the onions then let stand for 30 minutes.

2. Pour the onions on a colander and squeeze them to remove any liquid.

3. Combine the onions, cider vinegar, granulated sugar, mustard seeds, chili and turmeric in a pot. Bring the mixture to boil for 20 minutes.

4. The onions should be soft, and the liquid should have thickened.

5. Pack the relish in sterilized hot pint jars and cover with liquid. Leave a 1/2 inch headspace. Remove air bubbles and add more liquid if necessary.

6. Process the jars in hot water in the canner for 15 minutes. Put off the heat and let the jars stand in the canner for more 5 minutes before transferring them on a cooling rack.

Nutritional Information

Calories 420, Total fat 1g, Saturated fat 0g, Total carbs 98g, Net carbs 92g Protein 6g, Sugars 79g, Fiber 6g, Sodium 3590mg, Potassium 810mg

CHAPTER 11: Low- Sodium and Low-Sugar Recipes

Low-Sugar Cucumber slices

Make this mild, refreshing and an amazing cucumber slices with high water content. They ate delicious and many people serve it as savory food.

Prep time: 40 minutes, **Cook time:** 10 minutes, **Process time:** 10 minutes: **Serves** 5 pints

Ingredients

- 3-1/2 lb pickling cucumbers
- Boiling water
- 4 cups cider vinegar
- 3 cups splenda
- 1 tbsp canning salt
- 1 cup water
- 1 tbsp mustard seed
- 1 tbsp whole allspice
- 1 tbsp celery seed
- 4 1-inch cinnamon sticks

Preparation Method

1. Wash the cucumbers and cut off the blossom end. Discard.
2. Cut the cucumbers into 1/4 inch pieces thickness then pour boiling water over them. Let stand for 10 minutes. Drain the hot water and pour running cold water on the cucumbers. Drain the cucumber slices thoroughly.
3. Mix all other ingredients except cinnamon sticks in a stockpot and bring to boil. Add the cucumber slices and return to boil.
4. Place a cinnamon stick in each sterilized jar then using a slotted spoon, fill the jars with the hot cucumber pieces leaving a 1/2 inch headspace.
5. Remove any air bubbles then wipe the rims with a clean damp paper towel.

6. Process the jars in the pressure canner at 10 pounds pressure for 10 minutes.

Calories 17, Total fat 0.2g, Saturated fat 0g, Total carbs 3.1g, Net carbs 2.1g Protein 0.8g, Sugars 0g, Fiber 1g, Sodium 2.8mg, Potassium 193mg

Low- sugar Pickled Beets

This is an easy and delicious pickled beet recipe that everyone will love. Use pints with a wide mouth so that it's easy to pack the beets.

Prep time: 40 minutes, **Cook time:** 10 minutes, **Process time:** 10 minutes: **Serves** 8 pints

- 7 lb 2inch diameter beets
- 6 onions
- 6 cups apple cider vinegar
- 1 tbsp pickling salt
- 2 cups splenda
- 3 cups water
- 2 cinnamon sticks
- 12 whole garlic cloves

1. Trim the beet tops and leave an inch stem and roots. Wash the beet with clean water and cook in water for 30 minutes.
2. Cool the beets then trim off the stem and the roots. Slip off the skin then slice the beets into 1/4 inch slices.
3. Wash, peel and slice the onions into 1/4 inches.
4. Add vinegar, splenda and water in a Dutch oven. Tie garlic cloves and cinnamon sticks in a cheesecloth bag and add to the Dutch oven.
5. Bring the mixture to boil then reduce heat and simmer for 5 minutes. Remove the spice bag.
6. Pack the beets and onions in sterilized jars leaving a 1/2 inch headspace. Add the hot vinegar mixture but maintain the 1/2 inch headspace.
7. Remove the air bubbles and add more liquid if necessary. Wipe the jar rims and put the lids on.

8. Process the jars in the pressure canner at 10 pounds for 35 minutes.

9. Let the jars cool undisturbed for 12-24 hours before storing them in a cool dry place.

Calories 73, Total fat 0.3g, Saturated fat 0.1g, Total carbs 23.2g, Net carbs 18.7g Protein 0.1g, Sugars 29g, Fiber 4.5g, Sodium 108.1mg, Potassium 553mg

Low Sugar Canned Berry syrup

This is an easy to make, delicious berry syrup that is perfect for topping on pancakes or on icecream.

Prep time: 15 minutes, **Cook time:** 50 minutes, **Process time:** 10 minutes: **Serves** 5 pints

- 10-1/2 oz berries, fresh or frozen
- 4-1/2 cups apple juice
- 1-1/2 cups honey
- 1-1/2 cups sugar

1. Place the berries in a pot and crash them using a potato masher.

2. Add all other ingredients and bring them to boil at medium heat. Stir the mixture to ensure it doesn't overflow the pot.

3. Reduce heat such that the mixture keeps on boiling over the next 40 minutes. The mixture should have reduced by half and thickened.

4. Fill sterilized jars with the syrup leaving a 1/2 inch headspace. Wipe the jar rims and place the lids on.

5. Place the jars in the pressure canner with water such that the jars are covered by water at least 2-inches.

6. Cover the pressure canner with an ordinary lid that fits well and process the jars for 10 minutes.

7. Remove the lid and let the jars rest in the canner for 5 minutes before transferring them to a cooling rack.

8. Label the jars before storing in a cool dry place

Nutritional Information

Calories 51, Total fat 1g, Saturated fat 0.6g, Total carbs 13g, Net carbs 12g Protein 1g, Sugars 12g, Fiber 1g, Sodium 1mg, Potassium 28mg

Enjoy this low sugar canned fresh peaches all year. It's easy to can , perfect for everyone and can be served over hot biscuits and buttered toast

Prep time: 15 minutes, **Cook time:** 10 minutes, **Process time:** 25 minutes: **Serves** 3 pints

Ingredients

- 4 cups peach pulp
- 1/4 cup bottled lemon juice
- 2 cups crushed pineapple, unsweetened and drained
- 2 cups sugar

Preparation Method

1. Wash peaches and drain them well. Peel them and remove pit.
2. Use a medium blade to grid them or use a fork to crush them. Place the crushed peaches on a 2-quart saucepan and cook over low heat while stirring until all juice is released.
3. Strain the peaches on cheesecloth and allow juice to drip for 15 minutes.
4. Measure 4 cups of the peaches juice and combine with peach pulp, lemon juice, pineapple, and sugar in a saucepan.
5. Bring to boil while stirring occasionally to avoid sticking. Pour the hot mixture in sterilized pint jars leaving a 1/4 inch headspace.
6. Use a clean damp cloth to wipe the jar rims and put on the lids.
7. Place the jars in the pressure canner with water such that the jars are covered by water at least 2-inches.
8. Cover the pressure canner with an ordinary lid that fits well and Process the pint jars for 25 minutes in the boiling water.
9. Remove the jars from the canner and cool overnight.

Nutritional Information

Calories 20, Total fat 0g, Saturated fat 0g, Total carbs 4g, Net carbs 3.5g Protein 0g, Sugars 2g, Fiber 0.5g, Sodium 140 mg

Low sugar Grape Jelly with liquid sweetener

This is an easy jelly to make using a half of sugar used in the standard jelly. It's a perfect gratifying gift during holidays.

Prep time: 10 minutes, **Cook time:** 10 minutes, **Process time:** 10 minutes: **Serves** 3 pints

Ingredients

- 2 tbsp gelatin powder
- 2 tbsp lemon juice
- 24 oz grape juice
- 2 tbsp artificial sweetener

Preparation Method

1. Mix gelatin with lemon juice and grape juice in a saucepan to soften it, then bring to a hard boil.

2. Let boil for 1 minute then remove from heat. Add the sweetener and stir until well combined.

3. Pour the hot liquid in sterilized pint jars leaving a 1/4 inch headspace

4. Use a clean damp cloth to wipe the jar rims and put on the lids.

5. Place the jars in the pressure canner with water such that the jars are covered by water at least 2-inches.

6. Cover the pressure canner with an ordinary lid that fits well and Process the pint jars for 10 minutes in the boiling water.

7. Remove the jars from the canner and cool overnight.

Nutritional Information

Calories 25, Total fat 0g, Saturated fat 0g, Total carbs 6g, Net carbs 6g Protein 0g, Sugars 5g, Fiber 0g

Low sodium sliced sweet pickles

This is a perfect way to enjoy pickles without the fear of too much salt. Despite that there are store bought pickles these homemade pickles are the best especially if you are a strict low sodium diet.

Prep time: 15 minutes, **Cook time:** 10 minutes, **Process time:** 15 minutes: **Serves** 4 pints

- 4 lb pickling cucumbers

Canning syrup

- 1-2/3 cups white vinegar, distilled
- 3 cups sugar
- 1 tbsp whole allspice
- 2-1/4 tbsp celery seed

Brining solution

- 1 quart white vinegar, distilled
- 1 tbsp pickling salt
- 1 tbsp mustard seed
- 1/2 cup sugar

1. Wash cucumbers and cut off the blossom end. Slice cucumber into 1/4 inch slices.
2. Add all the canning syrup ingredients and bring them to a boil. Keep the mixture hot.
3. Add all the brining ingredients in a kettle then add the cucumber slices. Bring to boil until the cucumbers change color to dull green. Drain them.
4. Pack the cucumber slices in sterilized pint jars leaving a 1/2 inch headspace. Add the hot syrup and remove any air bubble. Add more syrup if necessary.
5. Use a clean damp cloth to wipe the jar rims and put on the lids.
6. Place the jars in the pressure canner with water such that the jars are covered by water at least 2-inches.
7. Cover the pressure canner with an ordinary lid that fits well and Process the pint jars for 15 minutes in the boiling water.
8. Cool the jars overnight before storing them in a cool dry place.

Calories 40, Total fat 0g, Saturated

fat 0.6g, Total carbs 10g, Net carbs 9g Protein 0g, Sugars 0g, Fiber 1g, Sodium 210mg, Potassium 30mg

Low sodium sweet dill pickles

This is a classic dill pickles recipe that will blow your mind away. The pickles are delicious and perfect for the healthy low sodium diet.

Prep time: 15 minutes, **Cook time:** 50 minutes, **Process time:** 10 minutes: **Serves** 8 pints

Ingredients

- 4 lb pickling cucumbers
- 6 cups vinegar
- 6 cups sugar
- 2 tbsp canning salt
- 1-1/2 tbsp celery seeds
- 2 onions, thinly sliced
- 8 heads fresh dill

Preparation Method

1. Wash the cucumbers, cut the blossom end, discard it and slice the cucumber into 1/4 inch slices.
2. Combine all other ingredients except onions and dill in a saucepan and bring the mixture to a boil.
3. Place a slice of onion and 1/2 head dill in each sterilized pint jar the pour the hot syrup on top leaving a 1/4 inch headspace.
4. Remove air bubbles and add more syrup if necessary. Use a clean damp cloth to wipe the jar rims and put on the lids.
5. Place the jars in the pressure canner with water such that the jars are covered by water at least 2-inches.
6. Cover the pressure canner with an ordinary lid that fits well and Process the pint jars for 20 minutes in the boiling water.
7. Cool the jars overnight before storing them in a cool. Dark and dry place.

Nutritional Information

Calories 51, Total fat 1g, Saturated fat 0.6g, Total carbs 13g, Net carbs 12g Protein 1g, Sugars 12g, Fiber 1g, Sodium 1mg, Potassium 28mg.

Low Sugar Canned honey and Cinnamon peaches

This is a tasty recipe that doesn't disappoint. Enjoy it all winter long with ice cream and oatmeal for breakfast.

Prep time: 20 minutes, **Cook time:** 5 minutes, **Process time:**30 minutes: **Serves** 7 pints

Ingredients

- 3 lb ripe peaches
- 1 cup honey
- 7 cinnamon sticks

Preparation Method

1. Peel the peaches and dunk them in boiling water for 2 minutes. The skin will come off.
2. Meanwhile, mix 9 cups of water and honey, and then bring the mixture to a boil over medium heat.
3. Remove the pits from the peaches and cut them into quarters.
4. Place a cinnamon stick in each sterilized pint jars. Pack the peaches in the jars and add the honey mixture leaving a 1/2 inch headspace.
5. Wipe the jar rims and adjust the lids.
6. Place the jars in the pressure canner with water such that the jars are covered by water at least 2-inches.
7. Cover the pressure canner with an ordinary lid that fits well and Process the pint jars for 30 minutes in the boiling water.

Nutritional Information

Calories 148, Total fat 0g, Saturated fat 0g, Total carbs 38.9g, Net carbs 12g Protein 0.1g, Sugars 38g, Fiber 0.2g, Sodium 7mg, Potassium 55mg

Low sugar pears

If you have a bumper crop of pears in your garden this season, you can't miss on making these overwhelming canned pears

Prep time: 20 minutes, **Cook time:** 0 minutes, **Process time:** 25 minutes: **Serves** 7 pints

Ingredients

- 10lb ripe pears
- Water
- Lemon juice

Preparation Method

1. Wash the pears and cut them into quarters.
2. Mix 1/2 cup of lemon juice with a gallon of water and the pears in the water for 3 minutes to prevent discouralation.
3. Pack the pears in sterilized pint jars and add boiling water leaving a 1/2 inch headspace.
4. Wipe the jar rims and adjust the lids.
5. Place the jars in the pressure canner with water such that the jars are covered by water at least 2-inches.
6. Cover the pressure canner with an ordinary lid that fits well and Process the pint jars for 25 minutes in the boiling water.
7. Let cool for 25 hours before storing in a cool dry place.

Nutritional Information

Calories 50, Total fat 0g, Saturated fat 0g, Total carbs 14g, Net carbs 13g Protein 0g, Sugars 5g, Fiber 1g, Sodium 0mg, Potassium 50mg

Reduced sugar pears in maple syrup

These maple infused pears are insanely delicious and addictive they are easy to make right in your kitchen. It's a thrilling addition to your pantry that will please everyone.

Prep time: 20 minutes, **Cook time:** 5 minutes, **Process time:** 30 minutes: **Serves** 7 pints

Ingredients

- 4 lb ripe and firm pears
- Water
- Lemon juice
- Hot maple syrup

1. Cut the pears in halves and remove the seeds.
2. Soak the pears in a gallon of water mixed with lemon and let rest for 3 minutes.
3. Pack the pears in sterilized pint jars then add hot maple syrup leaving a 1/2 inch headspace.
4. Wipe the jar rims and adjust the lids.
5. Place the jars in the pressure canner with water such that the jars are covered by water at least 2-inches.
6. Cover the pressure canner with an ordinary lid that fits well and Process the pint jars for 25 minutes in the boiling water.
7. Let cool for 25 hours before storing in a cool dry place.

Nutritional Information

Calories 40, Total fat 0g, Saturated fat 0g, Total carbs 10g, Net carbs 8g Protein 0g, Sugars 7g, Fiber 2g, Sodium 5mg, Potassium 60mg

Brandied Honey and Spice Pears

These deliciously sweet and spicy pressure canned pears are a perfect side for any meal. The best part is they can last for a year

Prep time: 35 minutes, **Cook time:** 5 minutes, **Process time 60 minutes: Serves** 6 pints

Ingredients

- 6 lb pears, ripe and firm
- Ascorbic acid color keeper
- 4 cups apple juice, cranberry juice, or apple cider
- 1/2 cup lemon juice
- 1-1/2 cups honey
- 3 tbsp crystallized ginger
- 8 inches stick cinnamon, break the sticks into halves
- 1/2 tbsp whole cloves
- 1/4 cup brandy

Preparation Method

1. Peel the pears and cut them into halves, then place them in the ascorbic acid to prevent the pears from discoloring. Set aside.
2. Make syrup in a 6-8 quart pot by combining apple juice, lemon juice, honey, ginger, cinnamon, and cloves. Bring the mixture to boil while constantly stirring. Reduce t the heat to low.
3. Drain the pears and add them to the syrup. Stir in brandy then increase the heat until the mixture is boiling. Reduce heat once more and simmer while stirring occasionally for 5 minutes or until the pears are almost tender.
4. Use a slotted spoon to pack the spears in clean pint canning jars ensuring you leave a half-inch headspace.
5. Ladle the syrup over pears and maintain the half-inch headspace. Use a clean towel to wipe the pint jar rims and put the lids on.
6. Load the jars into the pressure canner and process them at 10 pounds of pressure.
7. Allow the pressure in the canner

to drop to zero, remove the lid and lift the jars to a wire rack. Let them cool undisturbed for 24 hours before transferring them to a cool dry place.

Nutritional Information

Calories 262, Total fat 0g, Saturated fat 0g, Total carbs 67g, Net carbs 61g Protein 1g, Sugars 55g, Fiber 6g, sodium 5 mg, Potassium 253mg

Pressure Canned Apple Pie Filling with Maple and Cinnamon

Are you tired of store bought pie fillings? Make this homemade Apple filling and pressure can it so that its ready whenever you need to make a delicious pie

Prep time: 25 minutes, **Cook time:** 5 minutes, **Process time** 70 minutes: **Serves** 6 pints

Ingredients

- 1 lemon, cut into halves
- 10 pounds cooking apples, medium size
- 5 cups sugar
- 1-1/2 cup regular clear jel starch
- 2 tbsp cinnamon, ground
- 1 tbsp salt
- 5 cups apple juice
- 2-1/2 cup cold water
- 18 oz maple syrup
- 3/4 cup lemon juice

Preparation Method

1. Fill 2 large mixing bowls with cold water then squeeze 1/2 a lemon in each bowl.
2. Core and slice the apples into 3/4 inch wedges while putting them in the lemon water.
3. Drain the apples and measure 24 cups of water in a pot and boil it. Cook the apples; 1/4 at a time in the boiling water for 30 seconds.
4. Use a slotted spoon to remove the apples from the boiling water to another bowl. Cover the bowl to keep the apples hot and discard the cooking liquid.
5. Add sugar, clear jel starch, cinnamon and salt in the pot. Add the apple juice, water, and

maple syrup. Stir well

6. Stir cook over medium heat or until the mixture bubbles and thickens. Stir in lemon juice and let boil for 1 minute.
7. Stir in apple pieces until well coated.
8. Pack the apples in the sterilized jars leaving a 1-1/4 -inch headspace. Wipe the jar rims and place the lids and the rings.
9. Transfer the jars in a pressure canner and process for 70 minutes at 10 pounds pressure.
10. Allow the pressure in the canner to drop to zero, remove the lid and lift the jars to a wire rack. Let them cool undisturbed for 24 hours before transferring them to a cool dry place.

Nutritional Information

Calories 171, Total fat 0g, Saturated fat 0g, Total carbs 44g, Net carbs 42g Protein 0g, Sugars 36g, Fiber 2g, Sodium 52mg, Potassium 146mg

Canned Green Tea Chai-Spiced Peaches

These pressure canned chai spiced peaches are delicious when served straight from the jar. They are a mouthwatering dessert and a perfect pancake topper.

Prep time: 60 minutes, **Cook time:** 5 minutes, **Process time 60 minutes: Serves** 12 pints

Ingredients

- 15 pounds ripe peaches
- 4-1/2 cups water
- 1-1/3 cup sugar, granulated
- 1/2 cup brown sugar, packed
- 3 inch piece ginger, fresh peeled and thinly sliced
- 3inches stick cinnamon
- 10 garlic cloves
- 10 green cardamom pods
- 10 black peppercorns
- 1 tbsp green tea leaves, loose

Preparation Method

1. Bring a large pot of water into boiling. Cook the peaches, in batches, in the boiling water for 30-60 seconds or until the skin

starts to peel.

2. Use a slotted spoon to remove the pitches from the hot water to a large bowl of ice cold water. Remove the peaches from cold water and peel the skin.
3. Cut them into half lengthwise and discard the pits.
4. Combine, 4-1/2 cups water, both sugars, , ginger, cinnamon, garlic cloves, cardamom pods and peppercorns in a Dutch oven
5. Stir cook over medium heat until all the sugar has dissolved. Bring to boil then reduce heat and simmer for 20 minutes.
6. Remove from heat and stir in the green tea leaves. Cover and let rest for 5 minutes. Use a strainer to strain the syrup. Discard the solids.
7. Pack the peaches in the sterilized jars the ladle the syrup in each jar leaving a 1/2 inch headspace.
8. Wipe the rims, place the lids and place the rings on the jars. Process the jars for 60 minutes at 10 pounds pressure.
9. Wait for the canner to cool to remove the jars. Cool them on a wire rack before storing them.

Calories 69, Total fat 0g, Saturated fat 0g, Total carbs 17g, Net carbs 15g Protein 1g, Sugars 16g, Fiber 2g, Sodium 1mg, Potassium 189mg

Pressure Canned Pickled Plums

Plums have a short window of availability compared to any other fruits. That is why you should stock your kitchen pantry with these canned pickled plums.

Prep time: 35 minutes, **Cook time:** 20 minutes, **Process time:** 40 minutes: **Serves** 5 pints

Ingredients

- 3-1/2 lb red/ green or purple plums
- 2 onions
- 2 cups water
- 2 cups red wine vinegar
- 2-1/2 cups sugar
- 3 inches cinnamon sticks
- 8 whole allspice
- 4 garlic cloves

- 1/2 tbsp salt
- 2 star anise

Preparation Method

1. Wash the plums thoroughly with water and rinse them.
2. Trim off the roots and stems from the onions then cut them into 1/2 inch pieces.
3. Pack the plums and onions in sterilized jars.
4. Combine water, wine vinegar in a saucepan and bring the mixture to a boil. Stir in sugar, cinnamon sticks, allspice, garlic cloves, salt and star anise in a saucepan and let the mixture boil until the sugar has dissolved. Remove the mixture from heat.
5. Pour the hot mixture on the jars with plums leaving a 1/4 inch headspace.
6. Wipe the jar rims, place the lids and rings on the jar. Process the jars in the pressure canner for 40 minutes at 10 pounds pressure.
7. Wait for the pressure canner to depressurize to zero before removing the jars and cooling them on a wire rack for 12-24 hours.

Nutritional Information

Calories 239, Total fat 0g, Saturated fat 0g, Total carbs 59g, Net carbs 57g Protein 1g, Sugars 56g, Fiber 2g, Sodium 102mg, Potassium 252mg

Canned Spicy Ginger Red Hot Pears

Spoon this pressure canned spicy pears over your angel food cake, pound cake or on ice cream. It's a real crowd pleaser dessert when served on a fall night dinner.

Prep time: 20 minutes, **Cook time:** 5 minutes, **Process time:** 70 minutes: **Serves** 6 pints

Ingredients

- 6 lb ripe pears
- Ascorbic acid color keeper

- 4-1/2 cups water
- 2 cups sugar
- 6 cinnamon sticks
- 6 tbsp ginger, freshly chopped
- 12 tbsp red cinnamon candies.

Preparation Method

1. Peel the pears, cut them into halves, core them and cut into small wedges placing them in ascorbic acid.
2. Prepare the syrup by combining water and sugar in a heavy saucepan. Stir cook until all the sugar has dissolved.
3. Drain the pears into the saucepan with the syrup. Let boil then reduce heat to simmer for 4 minutes while uncovered.
4. Place a cinnamon stick in each jar, a tablespoon of ginger, and 2 tablespoon of cinnamon candied in each sterilized jar.
5. Ladle the pears in each jar leaving a 1/2 inch headspace. Wipe the rims, place the lids and place the rings on the jars.
6. Process the jars in the pressure canner for 70 minutes at 10 pounds pressure. Let the canner cool completely before removing the jars and cooling them on a wire rack.

Nutritional Information

Calories 122, Total fat 0g, Saturated fat 0g, Total carbs 32g, Net carbs 29g Protein 0g, Sugars 25g, Fiber 3g, Sodium 3mg, Potassium 105mg

Pressure Canned Honey-Lavender Peaches

Pressure can these peaches and get to enjoy a peaches flavored delicately with honey and a dash of lavender all year.

Prep time: 60 minutes, **Cook time:** 5 minutes, **Process time 70 minutes: Serves** 12 pints

Ingredients

- 15 lb ripe peaches
- 4 cups water
- 1-3/4 cups honey
- 2/3 cup Riesling
- 1 tbsp lavender buds, dried
- 1/2 tbsp salt
- 1 lemon

1. Bring a large pot of water into boiling. Cook the peaches, in batches, in the boiling water for 30-60 seconds or until the skin starts to peel.
2. Use a slotted spoon to remove the pitches from the hot water to a large bowl of ice cold water. Remove the peaches from cold water and peel the skin.
3. Cut them into half lengthwise and discard the pits.
4. Make the syrup by combining 4 cups of water, honey, Riesling, lavender buds and salt in a large saucepan. Stir cook over medium high heat until the honey has all dissolved.
5. Cut 3 inches strips of lemon peel using a vegetable peeler. Reserve the lemon for other use.
6. Pack the peaches in the jars with the cut side down. Add the lemon peel then ladle the syrup evenly among the jars leaving a 1/2 inch headspace.
7. Wipe the jar rims, and place the lids and rings on the jars. Transfer the jars to the pressure canner and process at 10 pounds pressure for 70 minutes.
8. Let the canner rest to cool before removing the jars and placing them on a rack to cool.

Nutritional Information

Calories 77, Total fat 0g, Saturated fat 0g, Total carbs 19g, Net carbs 17g Protein 1g, Sugars 18g, Fiber 2g, Sodium 22mg, Potassium 213mg

Pressure Canned Caramel Apple Butter

This pressure canned caramel apple butter is an irresistibly delicious dessert to serve your family all year and is a perfect homemade gift for holidays.

Prep time: 45 minutes, **Cook time:** 2 hours 20 minutes, **Process time 30 minutes: Serves** 6 pints

Ingredients

*   4-1/2 lb tart cooking apples
*   3cups apple cider
*   1-1/2 cups brown sugar, packed
*   1/2 cup granulated sugar
*   2 tbsp lemon juice

- 1/2 tbsp ground cinnamon

Preparation Method

1. Cut the apples into quarters, core them and add them to a 10 quart pot. Add apple cider and bring to boil. Reduce heat and simmer while stirring frequently for 35 minutes while covered.
2. Press the apple mixture through a sieve into a large bowl then discard the seeds and the peels. Measure a 7-1/2 cup of the pulp and return back to the pot.
3. Add in all other ingredients and bring the mixture to boil. Reduce heat and simmer uncovered for 1-3/4 hours or until the mixture is thick.
4. Ladle the hot mixture in the sterilized jars leaving a 1/4 inch headspace. Wipe the rims and place the lids and the rings on the jars.
5. Process the jars for 30 minutes at 10 pounds pressure. Let the canner cool before removing the jars and placing them on a cooling rack.

Nutritional Information

Calories 28, Total fat 0g, Saturated fat 0g, Total carbs 7g, Net carbs 7g

Protein 0g, Sugars 6g, Fiber 0g, Sodium 0mg, Potassium 24mg

Canned Port and Cinnamon Plums

Cinnamon plums with a splash of ruby port make this dish an amazing and standing out all-time dessert. Serve the plums piled on ice cream or on yogurt for the most elegant dessert ever.

Prep time: 25 minutes, **Cook time:** 10 minutes, **Process time:** 70 minutes: **Serves** 7 pints

Ingredients

- 4-1/2 lb plums
- 1 orange
- 4 cups water
- 2-1/2 cups sugar
- 3/4 cup ruby port
- 1/4 tbsp salt
- 7 3-inch cinnamon sticks

1. Quarter the plums and pit them. Cut 3 inches of strips from the orange peel. Squeeze 1/3 cup of juice from the orange
2. Make the syrup by adding the orange juice in a saucepan then add all other ingredients except the cinnamon sticks. Bring the mixture to boil and stir to dissolve all sugar.
3. Pack the plums, orange strips and cinnamon sticks in the sterilized jars. Ladle the syrup leaving a 1/2 inch headspace. Wipe the rims; place the lids and the rings on the jars.
4. Process the jars in the pressure canner for 70 minutes at 10 pounds pressure.
5. Let the pressure canner depressurize to zero to remove the jars. Transfer the jar to a wire rack and let cool for 24 hours before storing them.

Nutritional Information

Calories 125, Total fat 0g, Saturated fat 0g, Total carbs 30g, Net carbs 29g Protein 1g, Sugars 28g, Fiber 1g, Sodium 26mg, Potassium 135mg

Pressure Canned Tomatoes

If you have a pretty big harvest of tomatoes, don't let your fresh tomatoes go to waste. Preserve the extra tomatoes in jars to use all through the year.

Prep time: 15 minutes, **Cook time:** 0 minutes, **Process time:** 90 minutes: **Serves** 6 pints

Ingredients

- 9 lb ripe tomatoes
- Lemon juice
- salt

Preparation Method

1. Peel the tomatoes and cut them into halves.
2. Pack the tomatoes in the sterilized jars while pressing them down so that the space between the tomato pieces is filled with their juices.

3. Leave a 1/2 inch headspace. Add 1 tablespoon of lemon juice and 1/2 tablespoons of salt to each jar.
4. Wipe the rims and place the lids and the rings on the jars. Process them in the pressure canner for 90 minutes at 10 pounds pressure.
5. Wait the pressure canner to depressurize to remove the jars. Place the jars on a cooling rack then store them in a cool dry place.

Nutritional Information

Calories 13, Total fat 0g, Saturated fat 0g, Total carbs 3g, Net carbs 2g Protein 1g, Sugars 2g, Fiber 1g, Sodium 4mg, Potassium 170mg

Canned Apple Jam

This homemade apple jam is an exemplary topping to toast, ice cream, and in dinner rolls. Pressure can the apple jam to enjoy it even during off season.

Prep time: 90 minutes, **Cook time:** 5 minutes, **Process time:** 60 minutes: **Serves** 6 pints

Ingredients

- 4 lb tart apples
- 2 tbsp lemon juice
- 1-1/4 cups water
- 3 cups sugar, granulated
- 1 cup brown sugar, packed
- 1 tbsp vanilla
- 1 tbsp butter

Preparation Method

1. Combine apples, lemon juice, and 1/2 cup of water in a shallow saucepan and heat over medium-high heat. Bring to boil while stirring frequently then reduce heat to simmer for 30 minutes. The apples should be tender.
2. Press the apples through a sieve until you get 5 cups of the pulp. Discard the seeds and the peels.
3. Meanwhile, pour granulated sugar on a heavy saucepan and heat it over high heat as you shake the pan. When the sugar has started to melt, reduce heat, and cook on low heat for 10

minutes or until all the sugar has melted.

4. Remove the melted sugar from heat and add 3/4 cup of water. Return back to the heat and stir cook over medium heat until all sugar has dissolved.

5. Add the apple pulp and brown sugar to the mixture. Cook over medium-high heat until all caramel and sugar has dissolved.

6. Let the mixture boil gently for 10 minutes or until it thickens. Remove from heat and stir in vanilla and butter.

7. Ladle the jam in sterilized jars leaving a 1/4 inch headspace. Wipe jar rims and place the lids and the rings on the jars.

8. Process the jars for 55 minutes at 10 pounds pressure. Let the pressure canners depressurize before removing the jars. Place the jars on a rack undisturbed for 12-24 hours, then store them in a cool dry place.

Nutritional Information

Calories 57, Total fat 0g, Saturated fat 0g, Total carbs 14g, Net carbs 13g Protein 0g, Sugars 13g, Fiber 1g, Sodium 3mg, Potassium 31mg

APPENDIX: Measurement Conversion Chart

Attitude Feet	Weighted Gauge	Dial Gauge
0 – 1,000	10	11
1,001 – 2,000	15	11
2,001 – 4,000	15	12
4,001 – 6,000	15	13
6,001 – 8,000	15	14
8,001 – 10,000	15	15

www.ingramcontent.com/pod-product-compliance
Lightning Source LLC
Chambersburg PA
CBHW080905160726
48000CB00009B/2863